Ordinary Days

Ordinary Days

Family Life in a Farmhouse

DORCAS SMUCKER

Good Books

Intercourse, PA 17534
800/762-7171
www.GoodBks.com

To Paul,
Always there, always supportive, always loving.

Acknowledgments

I appreciate the many people who helped bring about this book: Ilva Hertzler, who wrote to *The Register-Guard* editor, urging him to feature me as a regular columnist. And, on the strength of that one letter, he did. Grant Podelco, my first editor at *The Register-Guard,* who accepted an unknown writer and shepherded me with the greatest kindness. Mark Johnson, my second editor, who pretty much let me have my own way. I always appreciate people who do that. Jessica Maxwell, who likes to say that she is pathologically helpful. I was blessed to be on the receiving end of your generosity. The Red Moons Writers' Group, who gave me valuable insights and believed in me. I hope I can help you as much as you've helped me.

My deepest thanks to Paul, Matt, Amy, Emily, Ben, and Jenny. You love and encourage me, laugh at all the right places, and let me write about you. Steven, you joined our family after this book was written, and you brought us wonder and joy. And thanks to God: you are the gracious giver of all good gifts.

Credits

All the essays in this book were published in *The Register-Guard,* Eugene, Oregon, except for "Traditions," which previously appeared in *Generations,* the newsletter of the Retired Senior Volunteer Program in Albany, Oregon. All of the essays in this book, except for "Emily's Song," "Aunts," "Oregon Coast," "Judgment Day," and "Escapes," appeared in an earlier book, titled *Ordinary Days: Letters from Harrisburg,* by Dorcas Smucker.

Scripture references on pages 17, 143 (first reference), 144 (first reference), and 145 are taken from the HOLY BIBLE, KING JAMES VERSION. Scripture references on pages 47, 135, 139, 143 (second reference), and 144 (second and third references) are taken from the HOLY BIBLE, NEW INTERNATIONAL VERSION® NIV®. Copyright © 1973, 1978, 1984 by International Bible Society. Used by permission of Zondervan. All rights reserved.

Cover art and design by Wendell Minor
Design by Dawn J. Ranck

ORDINARY DAYS
Copyright © 2006 by Good Books, Intercourse, PA 17534
International Standard Book Number-13: 978-1-56148-522-2
International Standard Book Number-10: 1-56148-522-5

Library of Congress Catalog Card Number: 2006005149

Library of Congress Cataloging-in-Publication Data

Smucker, Dorcas.
Ordinary days : family life in a farmhouse / Dorcas Smucker.
    p. cm.
ISBN-13: 978-1-56148-522-2 (pbk.)
    1. Country life—Oregon—Willamette River Valley—Anecdotes. 2. Smucker, Dorcas—Family—Anecdotes. 3. Willamette River Valley (Or.)—Social life and customs—Anecdotes. 4. Willamette River Valley (Or.)—Biography—Anecdotes. 5. Schmucker family—Anecdotes. I. Title.
F882.W6S55 2006
979.5'3—dc22   2006005149

Table of Contents

Introduction

My relatives were wonderful storytellers. *Fertsayluh* they called it in Pennsylvania German—the art of spinning tales and of seeing the quirky and unusual in the most ordinary events.

At family reunions, my Aunt Vina would mesmerize us with stories of how Grandma cured warts or the time the cat ate the dishrag. Even if we had heard the story a dozen times before, we always savored that same delicious waiting as the story progressed and anticipated that expertly timed ending when the room exploded in laughter.

I don't *fertsayle* much at family gatherings, but I like to think that I learned from my relatives to see the profound and the humorous in simple things. I have many opportunities to do so, living with a husband and six children in a 95-year-old farmhouse in Oregon's Willamette Valley.

This book is a collection of stories about our lives, telling of simple blessings and ordinary days. Many of these stories refer to our five children. After this book was written, we welcomed a sixth child into our family: Steven, an active, imaginative, 10-year-old boy from Kenya.

These essays do not appear in chronological order, and they are meant to be sipped one at a time like a mid-morning cup of tea, rather than devoured in one sitting like Thanksgiving dinner. I hope they will echo in your own life, reminding you of family times, lessons learned, and God's loving touch on all of us.

Family

Expecting the Unexpected

*O*ne of the first things I noticed about my friend's house, when I stopped in last Christmas, was that her Nativity set looked like it hadn't moved an inch from where she first set it weeks before. This friend, I should add, doesn't have children.

I have five children and, at my house, I never knew what my Nativity set would be doing when I walked into the living room. Sometimes I found Joseph and the shepherds lying on their backs because 1-year-old Jenny thought they needed to go night-night. At other times, I've found my 10-year-old using the figures to act out the Christmas story, with Mary pinch-hitting as a wise man and riding off on the camel.

I can't help but compare my friend's life, with its order and routine, to mine, with its constant unpredictability.

When our first child was born, I didn't know what to expect in my new role as a mom. Fifteen years and four more children later, I still don't. This was a journey into the unknown, with unexpected curves in the road and surprises around each corner. Motherhood keeps me guessing, always a bit off balance, braced for a twist in the plot when things appear most predictable.

For one thing, I am often amazed at how much it hurts to be a mom, from the pain of childbirth to the sick, bottomless ache when a child is lost. Even more, I am stunned by the joy—when I hold each child for the first time, when the lost ones are found, when I get a hug from a difficult child when I least expect it.

Another unexpected twist is the questions. I always knew that young children ask a lot of questions. What I didn't expect was when, where, and on what subjects. The most startling ones were hissed in my ear when I was absorbed in the sermon at church.

"Mom! Do you have a baby in your tummy or are you just fat?"

"Did you know the Blackbird airplane flies so high that the pilots have to wear space suits?"

In addition, there are what I call Clear Blue Sky questions, which pop out with no preliminaries.

"Did we go opposite of the other people?"

"How does Becky hold carrots?"

"What's that stuff beside the other stuff?"

Appearing out of nowhere, these questions make me dizzy, and I end up asking 10 or 15 questions myself before I figure out what they're talking about.

As a mom, my plans seldom work out like I think they will. My fear of snakes and crawly things is, I believe, a learned phobia, and I was determined not to pass it on to my children. So I let them read *National Geographic* books with explicit photographs of snakes and even took them through the reptile house at the zoo. "Oh, look at the pretty snakes," I gushed, and tried not to let them see me shudder.

I was successful: none of my children is afraid of snakes. But I was much more successful than I planned to be. Matt wants a snake for a pet, and Emily sits in the garden and drapes earthworms over her hands. One day, when the baby was fussy, Amy gave her a rubber snake to chew on. I turned around and there she was, blissfully gnawing. I gasped, horrified, and thought, *This wasn't what I had in mind at all. All I wanted was for them not to be afraid to walk through tall grass.*

My family, I found, doesn't fit into the experts' easy models. Discipline, according to the books, is supposed to fit a formula: clear instruction plus logical consequences would equal disciplined kids and satisfied parents. One spring I bought an expensive rainbow-colored stamp pad for making greeting cards. I knew my daughters would want to use it, so I gave them clear instructions.

"You can use this, but when you're finished you always slide this little knob over here so the colors don't run together, and you always put the cover back on so it doesn't dry out. Do you understand?"

They understood.

A few days later, I stopped by my rubber-stamp desk and there was my new stamp pad, cover off, colors bleeding together. Nine-year-old Emily was the culprit, I soon found out.

"Do you realize how much I paid for this thing?" I ranted. "And I told you to take care of it, and you didn't, so you won't be allowed to use it anymore."

Emily looked at me with big, blue, tear-filled eyes. "I'm sorry, Mom." Then she added softly, "I used it to make a Mother's Day card for you."

Then there was the day when I had four children under nine years old and we were all having a bad day. Everyone was grouchy and uncooperative. Nothing I did seemed to change things, so, even though I knew better, I tried to fall back on guilt.

"I feel like quitting!" I announced dramatically. "Nobody likes me. Nobody listens to me. Maybe I should just quit and let someone else be your mom."

Ordinary Days

There was a brief silence and then my 4-year-old chirped, "Okay! I want Aunt Bonnie to be my mom!"

Someone certainly went on a guilt trip, but it wasn't any of the children.

On another bad day a few years later, I wasn't happy with how I handled things. That evening I sank into a chair in the living room and moaned to my husband, "Please tell me I'm a good mom."

Paul can be expected to indulge me even if he has to stretch the truth. He managed to sound sincere as he assured me that yes, I'm a good mom. What I didn't expect was the sudden chorus of little voices agreeing with him.

"Yeah, Mom, you're a good mom."

"You are, really."

"I think you're a good mom."

Things don't stay put at my house, my plans seldom work out, and I never know what to expect from one minute to the next. But, all things considered, I wouldn't trade this job for anything.

Matt Learns to Drive

My son Matt seems 4 years old again, walking from my parents' house to his cousin Leonard's next door. He grows smaller and smaller on that long, dusty lane as I watch from the porch.

He is 7, calmly posing for a photograph while he waits for his ride on his first day of school, then asking sweetly, "Now would you like me to take a picture of you crying?"

And he's 11, calling, "Mom, look at me!" from 70 feet up a Douglas fir at Alsea Falls. And I, forcing myself to stay calm, am shouting back, "If you fall out of there and break both legs, don't come running to me!"

And now he's 15, counting the days until he gets his driver's license.

Matt has always had a tall-tree-and-lightning relationship with disaster. He imitated Calvin and Hobbes, washed a disposable diaper with a load of black jeans, and almost set the house on fire with his scientific experiments. He needed ipecac, tetanus boosters, and emergency surgery.

When he learned to drive, I only imagined more disasters. I pictured him on dark streets coming up on grandmas at crosswalks, and on I-5 making split-second decisions among wolf-packs of cars and semi trucks roaring behind him like charging bulls.

After he got his permit, the first time Matt drove the car was to church one evening, where he sailed down the driveway and kept going so fast that he almost hit the brick planter at the end of the parking lot. Even his mild-tempered dad raised his voice.

The next morning Matt drove the van to school, again with Paul supervising. He turned into the driveway, I was told later, and didn't straighten out the wheels but drove onto the grass, where he bounced along for 50 feet and then turned back onto the driveway while the other students at school and the sewing-circle women in a nearby church-fellowship hall watched in astonishment.

"Why did you do that?" everyone asked him later.

He had no idea.

I found that I couldn't chew gum while Matt drove, for fear I'd inhale it while sucking in air through my teeth. I also found myself leaning to the left, not politically, but literally, as though it would keep us from lurching off the edge as he hugged the white line on shoulderless country roads.

Paul let him drive on the freeway when we went on vacation. To me, it was sheer, terrifying lunacy to fly along at freeway speeds with the fate of our van, family, and vacation in Matt's uncertain hands. I finally convinced my husband of this—or so I thought. Then I heard him having a little man-to-man talk with Matt in the front seat, and it sounded suspiciously like, "Well, we both know you can drive perfectly well, but Mom is kind of scared, so let's humor her, shall we?"

"It's a guy thing," my sister told me later. "They love freeways and think they're the best place to train new drivers. My-father-in-law takes the freeways all over Seattle," she went on, "and my mother-in-law hates them and takes all these complicated back roads."

Drivers'-education classes started in October at Linn-Benton Community College in Albany. The teacher was a brisk, no-

nonsense woman who seemed capable and intimidating—just right for teaching this roomful of 15-year-olds to drive.

A parent was required to attend the first class, so I got to watch a gut-wrenching film about accidents involving newly-licensed drivers. The parents in the audience wiped their eyes. The teens didn't seem affected.

Every Monday night for six weeks, we made the half-hour drive to Albany, where I shopped or read for three hours until the class ended.

"A policeman showed us slides of accident scenes," Matt told me after one class. "One picture showed half a body over here and the other half 10 feet away."

I said, "Eeewww, how awful." I thought, *Yes! Bring it on. Whatever it takes.*

On the night of the final exam, Matt came to the car with a dejected look on his face. "How did you do?" I asked anxiously.

His shoulders slumped. "Flunked," he mumbled.

I admit, I screamed—thinking of all those hours and all that money wasted. Matt let me rant for about 30 seconds then sat up straight and grinned. "Just kidding, Mom. I actually did fine."

Then came the behind-the-wheel sessions, where I again dropped him off at the parking lot and hung around town for three hours, certain that every siren I heard involved my son.

Rain blasted down like a Minnesota thunderstorm the night of Matt's last lesson. I half expected his teacher to tell us that the session was postponed. But no, there she was, waiting in her car, smiling, even. I pictured myself riding with two 15-year-olds in the pouring rain, gathering darkness, and glaring streetlights. Never.

Afterward, Matt casually informed me that his instructor told him he was driving too fast and if he goes over the speed limit once—once!—he fails the course. He passed. I drove home in the storm and Matt—Matt?—kept asking me nervously to slow down.

After Christmas we took a trip to the Middle East to visit my sister. Matt loved to stand at her upstairs window and watch the traffic below. Battered white Toyotas wove in and out of traffic in a constant game of "chicken" and the only requirement for drivers, it seemed, was knowing how to honk the horn.

"Man, I wish my drivers'-ed teacher could see this," he kept saying. "She'd think I wasn't so bad after all."

Matt no longer sighs when I hand him newspaper clippings of accidents involving teenage drivers. He stays in the center of his lane and glances over his shoulder before changing lanes. Paul lets him drive in Eugene and tells me he does very well.

Sometimes my daughter wants to go to the library and I don't have time to take her. Or I'm making supper and discover I'm out of cheddar cheese. Then I think, with sudden, satisfying anticipation, *You know, Matt gets his license in only 26 days!*

Just Like Mom

I came home from a dentist appointment one Monday in March and found six lambs in my kitchen. Only a day old, baaing hungrily in cardboard boxes, these were "bummer" lambs whose mothers were unable to care for them.

As my husband mixed the milk and fed them, he explained that a call came unexpectedly that morning from the Oregon State University sheep barn. The lambs were available, but the little shed he was building for them in the orchard was only half finished.

Until the shed was finished the next day, the lambs stayed indoors. My 2-year-old daughter Jenny fell in love with them. She'd reach out hesitantly to pat their backs, then squeal wildly when they touched their cold noses to her arm.

I was cleaning up the kitchen after lunch when I heard a little voice behind me commanding, "Hold still! Now, blow your nose. Blow your nose!"

I turned around. There was Jenny, leaning over the side of a box, trying to hold a tissue to a lamb's nose. The lamb was shaking his head from side to side, and Jenny, getting more and more frustrated, was determinedly trying to wipe a bit of moisture off that small black nose.

The scene was adorable, of course—a pert little girl with red-gold curls trying to control a woolly, long-legged lamb that had no intention of cooperating. But the reason I stared, dumbfounded, was because in that moment I saw my mother in my earnest little daughter.

It was over 30 years ago, the spring that Dad traveled so much. We had a flock of sheep in a pasture across the creek, and whenever Dad left, the sheep immediately began giving birth. One evening we spent several hours penning up the new mothers in a shed and making sure the lambs were nursing.

I still remember the icy cold in the air that evening as we finished up and Mom, my sister Becky, and I left the shed to return to the house. We hadn't gone far when a sad-faced old ewe came wandering over to us, looking like she was begging for help. She obviously had a cold, with a terribly runny nose, which Becky and I thought was disgusting.

Mom, however, took one look at the ewe and pulled an old handkerchief out of her coat pocket. With a quick swipe, she reached out and wiped that awful slime off the sheep's nose. That was even more disgusting, I thought, but we all laughed anyway. The ewe looked grateful, and we walked on to the house.

Whatever quirky little gene inspired my mother to wipe a sheep's nose apparently lay hidden for a generation and then suddenly showed up on this Monday afternoon in my feisty 2-year-old.

I find it fascinating, these mysteries of mothers and daughters, of genes and generations. What is it that makes me repeat my mother's habits and patterns, or that makes bits of my mom show up, at the most unexpected moments, in myself and my daughters?

Shopping for comfortable shoes, I try on a pair, look down, and there I see an exact replica of my mother's ankles and feet. I glance in the mirror while braiding my daughter's hair, and there are my mother's hands, braiding my sister's long brown hair with the same firm strokes.

Even the circumstances around the lambs held an uncanny resemblance to Mom's experiences. Just a few days after we got the lambs, Paul had to leave for a 12-day trip to Mexico to visit several churches he oversees. I was left with the responsibility of mixing milk for the lambs and feeding them four times a day. Paul felt badly about adding to my duties, as he had hoped the lambs wouldn't arrive until after his trip.

When Dad left to do his research on Amish schools that spring in the 1960s, Mom no doubt felt some of the same resentment I did when her husband's project turned into another responsibility added to her enormous load. But I remember the rapturous smile on her face whenever she saw a new baby animal on the farm. I have a feeling that, like me, she found the newborn lambs irresistible as they braced their skinny legs and drank hungrily, their tails fluttering like a flag in a stiff wind.

On Sunday afternoons, my mother was always making scrapbooks to give away to elderly people or invalids. These were not the photo-album variety that are so popular now, but her own unique blend of pictures and Bible verses. She would scan magazines and junk mail for appropriate illustrations. Then she'd glue a picture on a scrapbook page and find a coordinating Bible verse to write underneath it. To this day, whenever I see a picture of mountain goats I immediately think, *"The high hills are a refuge for the wild goats"—Psalm 104:18.*

Our 11-year-old daughter Emily decided to make a book for Jenny's third birthday in April. She nosed through catalogs and magazines, then sat snipping and gluing at her desk, utterly absorbed and contented, a replica of Mom at the dining-room table on a Sunday afternoon. The result was a revision of "Little Miss Muffet" in which Little Miss Jenny sat on a penny and a bug gave her a hug.

Ordinary Days

"She's just like your mom," my husband told me, amazed, leafing through the book and looking at the cut-out, glued-in magazine pictures of a little girl, a bug, and the shoes Jenny wore to chase the bug away.

Mom is almost 82 years old, and the gradual loss of her sight is curbing her boundless creativity. Much as I hate to admit it, I know she won't always be with us. But I am comforted knowing that, years from now, I will turn around at unexpected moments and, in the mirror or in my daughters, I will catch a vivid glimpse of Mom.

Wallpaper Gifts

I believe we were on the third strip of wallpaper when I quit wondering what was wrong with our marriage.

Every year, with the flood of holiday advertisements, I find a nagging little question deep inside me: If our marriage is as solid as I think it is, why do Paul and I have such a hard time buying Christmas gifts for each other?

Surely, among all this excess of things, he should be able to direct me toward something he wants. Just one gift—we try to keep it simple. And not too specific—I like to surprise him. Hobby supplies? He likes birdwatching. What do you buy a birdwatcher who already has a bird book and binoculars? Should I get him a sweater? No, he can't reach the pens in his shirt pocket. He's not into gadgets, electronic toys, or music. He likes sports, but he doesn't need any equipment. Tools and computer programs are too specific. If I pick out something, it'll be the wrong thing. If he tells me what to get, there's no surprise.

"Which is it?" I ask him. "Are you so un-materialistic that nothing appeals to you, or do you buy everything you need?"

Probably both, he says calmly.

He is all science and logic. I am all impulse and emotion. And we don't know what to give each other.

I could think of a hundred things he could buy for me; he can't think of one. He wants a specific assignment, and I want to be surprised. Craft supplies? He is as ignorant of rubber stamps and needlework as I am of car repairs and carpentry. Clothes, I suggest, like a sweater or a new dress, and he gets a nervous look in his eyes. Last summer, he repaired a roof 90 feet off the ground. Last week, he killed a mouse that was caught, alive and clattering, in a trap in the kitchen cupboard. He would rather do both of those than navigate the ladies' clothing department at JCPenney.

"Why don't you buy me fabric for a dress?" I suggest. "Four yards. Then you don't have to worry about sizes."

"What if you don't like it?" he asks.

"I'll like it because you picked it out for me," I say, knowing that he doesn't understand this and probably never will.

And I worry about our marriage.

This year, the annual worries cropped up on Thanksgiving Day, when the newspaper came stuffed with sale flyers from almost every store in town. It was also the day that we wallpapered the kitchen. This odd combination came about because our invited guests didn't come for Thanksgiving dinner because of illness in the family, and we were on our own.

Paul, the family organizer, wanted to make sure we all had a special day despite the change in plans. For him, this meant going ahead with the big dinner. For the children, hours of table games. And me? I wanted to start and finish a big project.

"Like what?" Paul asked.

"Like papering the kitchen," I said, since the wallpaper I ordered had just arrived, and I was eager to transform our bare kitchen walls into something more colorful.

The children and I cooked a huge turkey dinner while Paul put up new smoke alarms, fixed the screen doors, and shaved three doors that always stick.

After we ate and cleaned up the kitchen, Paul and the children started playing Skip-Bo, while I gathered rolls of wallpaper and a container of water. I would put wallpaper on the lower 40 inches of the south half of the kitchen, I decided, then top it with a border. Then, I would put a border all the way around the top of the kitchen walls.

The work was a bit tedious, I found, but not difficult. I measured, cut, and soaked each strip, then flattened it against the wall, matched the blue flowers, and smoothed the paper with a wet rag. In the living room, Paul and the children worked through a wild game of Pit and a quieter Phase 10.

By the children's bedtime, I was ready to start on the upper border of wallpaper. I pictured myself, five-feet-three, up on the stepladder, fighting with 15 feet of slimy wallpaper, next to a nine-foot ceiling. This was a two-person job. Paul said he'd help. We put the children to bed and started in.

Things are sometimes tense when he gets involved in my projects, and this was no exception. I was ready to plunge the first roll of border into a bucket of water, but he insisted that there was a much more efficient way to do it, and began to fold the paper back and forth like a giant Christmas bow. I thought, but did not say, *Listen, is this my project or yours?*

He lowered the wallpaper bow into the water, let it soak for 10 seconds, and pulled it out. We were ready to attach it when I noticed the dry sections on the paper, every two feet. We headed back to the bucket as he admitted he was wrong, and I thought, but did not say, *I told you so.*

We tried again. He stood on the ladder and carefully fitted the paper into the corner and along the wall. I stood on a chair and played out the wet paper, not too loose, not too tight. Then he moved the ladder, I stood on it, and we both smoothed the paper with wet rags. The tension eased as, within a few minutes, we were working like a well-trained team.

I matched the flower pattern on the beginning of the second strip to the end of the first, and we moved slowly along the west wall of the kitchen. Up on the counter, down on a chair. He moved the ladder for me; I moved a chair for him. We both leaned over the refrigerator, trying to reach and smooth the last of the air bubbles out of the wallpaper.

Half done. Already the kitchen looked brighter, more cheerful. We started in one corner and I planned to keep going around the room, left to right, solving problems as I encountered them. But Paul, who sees the big picture, suggested that we backtrack and do the east wall next, from right to left, so that we would have a short end of wallpaper to fit around the chimney.

I am better with details, so before long I was standing precariously on the edge of the dishwasher, craning my neck, trying to fit the wallpaper around the chimney where Paul's great-grandpa built it crooked 90 years ago. To do this, I had to slit the wet paper with a razor blade and carefully overlap. I was sure that, as Garrison Keillor once said, I was going to fall over backwards if I had a serious thought in the back of my head. Paul didn't say, but I'm sure he thought, that my fears were completely illogical. Nevertheless, he stood on the floor behind me until I had finished, and helped me down.

By the fourth strip of wallpaper we were amazingly coordinated, inching along the kitchen counter and placing the wallpaper on the wall above the cupboards, tucking it into corners and smoothing it down. Last of all, I stood with one foot on the counter and one on the dishwasher, slicing off the extra wallpaper and matching the two ends. Then we were done. I hopped down and we high-fived in our beautifully transformed kitchen.

I was no longer worried about our marriage, or about gifts. Maybe I'd give him cashews for Christmas; maybe he'd give me socks. It didn't matter.

The best gifts are given daily, and I am daily surprised.

Emily's Song

My daughter Emily lay on our bed not long ago, propped on pillows, knitting her first tentative rows. I sat beside her, reading aloud from *James Herriot's Dog Stories*. The rest of the family was away at some activity that Emily was too sick to attend.

Staying in bed is unbearably boring for a 12-year-old, and the knitting and reading were my attempts to keep Emily occupied. But deep into the story of Tricki Woo, the Pekingese, I realized that we were actually having a good time—just the two of us, relaxing and having fun in a way that we would never have taken time for if she were well. Perhaps, after all, something good could come out of this long ordeal.

I didn't think too much of it when Emily got sick and missed more than a week of school at the end of the fifth grade. The flu and end-of-year stress, I figured.

She had frequent headaches over the summer and into the next school year. She also seemed to catch every cold and flu she was exposed to. We were soon in a frustrating cycle in which she would come home from school with piles of homework because, she said, she'd had another headache and couldn't study in school.

For a long time, I dealt with each symptom as it arose, doling out Tylenol, taking her temperature, trying to decide if she was well enough to go to school. I found her headaches and illnesses annoying. Was she making them up so she could stay home from school? Why couldn't she be more disciplined, more brave, more stoic?

Moms are sometimes the last ones to see the forest for the trees, and it was a long time before I finally stepped back, looked at Emily, and admitted that something was wrong.

While it was frightening to admit, it was also liberating. When her friends said, "Emily's sick again?" I could say, "Yes. We think something's wrong with her, and we're trying to find out what it is."

Few things are as painful as watching a child suffer, few things as trying to one's faith. For me, the most painful moment was one evening when Emily went to bed with an excruciating headache that nothing alleviated. When I went upstairs to bed, I heard her wispy voice coming out of the darkness in her room, singing "How Great Thou Art." I asked her why she was singing.

"Because there's nothing else to do," she said.

My own faith faltered sometimes, wanting an explanation that would all make sense, that would explain how a loving God could let a child suffer. But faith, finally, consists of trusting when there are no easy answers, singing in the dark because there's nothing else to do and finding it to be everything.

Emily was sick with the flu one evening, lying on the couch reading an *American Girl* magazine. She read a sad story of a girl whose parents were divorced. The girl had to spend alternate weeks with each parent.

"Maybe that's why I have to go through this," Emily said, "because God knows I'll never go through that and he wants me to sympathize with people who suffer."

While Emily was brave, grateful, and endlessly sweet when she was sick, I could always tell when she was recovering because she would tease her little sister until she screamed. My emotions were tangled enough without this added complication: As soon as she was well, Emily became a typically moody 12-year-old who tried my patience to the breaking point.

Having had two previous 12-year-olds, I knew another year or two would take care of most of the obnoxious behavior. But solutions for her physical problems were much harder to find.

Narrowing thousands of possible diagnoses and remedies down to one or two seemed impossible. While we researched all we could, most of the insights we gained were ones we stumbled across accidentally.

I was brushing Emily's hair one morning when she flinched and said, "Ouch! When you brush my hair, it makes that side of my head hurt more."

"That side of your head?" I said.

Yes, she said, her headaches were almost always on one side. So, in all likelihood, she had migraines. Not a pleasant diagnosis, but at least it narrowed our field ever so slightly.

We soon found that over-the-counter painkillers seldom worked. One day, impulsively, Emily picked up my cup of black tea and drank it. To our astonishment, her headache went away. It didn't always work, but it was a tiny step forward.

We kept a food diary and slowly, a few patterns emerged. MSG, a common flavor enhancer. Sugary things for breakfast.

But there were no long-term solutions, and Emily got worse instead of better.

I thought of dozens of possible causes. Did she have some terrible disease such as leukemia? Was it psychological, and she was being abused in secret by someone? Did I have that strange disorder where a mom subconsciously tries to make her child sick? Did she have the digestive disorders that run in my family?

We went to our family doctor, of course. The medical field, for all its efficiency with broken bones and ear infections, seems strangely helpless in the face of a chronic illness with vague symptoms.

"You'll have to experiment to see what triggers her headaches," the doctor told me. "If they persist, we might have to put her on a preventive medication all the time."

Twelve years old and dependent on a prescription medicine—that didn't appeal to me at all. So I hesitantly opened the door into the world of alternative medicine, feeling like one of the gullible acquaintances (whom we made fun of), who were always hunting down a new doctor or a new magic cure.

I didn't find chelation therapy or mineral baths, but I did find a remarkable variety of "natural" remedies.

I also found myself bombarded from every side with people who emerged from the woodwork with their own suggestions and cures.

"Acupuncture! It works wonders for migraines! But you have to get the right practitioner."

"You should get her eyes checked. My daughter had all these headaches and they quit as soon as she got glasses."

"Have you heard of essential oils? Here, listen to this tape and see what you think."

"Have you taken her to a chiropractor? I wonder if her neck is out of place."

"I really think you need Juice-Plus to build up her immune system."

"I wonder if she has allergies. I've noticed she has dark circles under her eyes."

"I have a wheat allergy and a lot of her symptoms sound like mine. There's a naturopath in Portland that I really like."

"Sugar in the morning gives her headaches? I'll bet it's her pancreas! Here, try these herbal pills."

Since most of these people gave suggestions rather than commands, we felt like there was a vast network of people who supported us, cared for us, and wanted to help.

Eventually, I found a doctor who understood my medical misgivings and my goal of finding the causes of Emily's problems. I talked to him on the phone one day when Emily had an unusually painful migraine.

"I'm wondering if we need to get a prescription painkiller," I said. "I gave her an adult dose of Excedrin Migraine and it's not doing a thing."

"Before we do that," the doctor said, "try this: Put her feet in hot water and put ice on her head."

I felt like the biblical Naaman dipping in the Jordan for his leprosy, but I hoisted Emily onto the bathroom counter, put her feet in a sinkful of hot water, and held a bag of frozen peas on her head.

Half an hour later, the migraine was down in the bearable range and she no longer had that agony in her eyes. It felt like a giant step forward.

As I write this, Emily has been well for a week, the longest stretch in several months. We continue to research, take blood tests, and monitor her diet. I am home schooling her, thus avoiding that tough decision every morning of whether or not she's well enough to go to school.

We savor the time we spend together and the people who show us they care.

And most of all, we never give up hope, even if it means singing in the dark, at times, because there's nothing else to do.

Two Babies

August, 1998—I'm pregnant. Paul and I are happy but realistic.

September—I lie curled up in bed and fight a terrible, constant nausea 24 hours a day. I get a phone call from Simone, who married Paul's cousin Darrell last May. "I'm pregnant," she says. "I'm happy, but I'm really sick."

I tell Simone the things I need to hear: This will pass. It will all be worth it. In the end, you'll have a baby.

October—Simone and I keep in touch. We share tips for survival—foods that stay down and how to brush our teeth without throwing up. I make the decision to take medication for the nausea. Simone chooses to tough it out with no medication.

Spring, 1999—Simone and I are back on our feet. I worry about our baby. I'm 36 years old, and I know my chances of having a baby with Down Syndrome increase with age. And the medication I took is supposed to be safe, but what if it isn't entirely? I ponder the fierce protectiveness I feel toward this child, this intense desire for everything to be normal. Is it for the baby's sake, or mine? I've heard that Downs babies have a single crease across the palm of the hand, instead of two creases going partway across, like the rest of us. I hope desperately for two creases.

April 21—I sit in a tub of water in our dining room, surrounded by Paul, my midwives, and a swirling cloud of pain. *I can't do this,* I think; *please get me out of here.* Suddenly, the agony vanishes and I'm holding my squirming, wet baby daughter.

Ordinary Days

There's nothing in the world like giving birth, nothing to match this relief and euphoria. Jennifer Anne is here and I love her completely. Awed, we inspect this wonderful little person. With my thumb, I pry open her little fist. Two creases. But I know now I would love her just as much with a single crease.

May, 1999—The new-baby adjustments are a hundred times easier with the fifth than with the first, I decide.

Simone's baby is due three weeks after Jenny. I wait for news—three weeks, four weeks, five. Finally, after six weeks, the phone call from Paul's mom: Darrell and Simone have a baby girl named Dawnisha. I sense in my mother-in-law's voice that this isn't the normal she's-here-and-everything's-fine phone call. I'm right. "But . . . ," she says, and I feel a fist in my stomach. Something's wrong; a few fingers missing; she's not entirely sure. They're taking the baby to a hospital in Portland.

Over the next few days, vague reports filter through the Smucker grapevine. It's not just fingers missing; there's something about her arms. And her face. How is Simone? we ask each other. And Darrell? No one seems to know, only that Simone doesn't want visitors. *What should we do?* we wonder. *What should we say?* Mostly we leave them alone with what must be a confusing mixture of joy and pain, and each of us grieves as well. I sit in my rocking chair and feed Jenny, stroking her perfect little hands and weeping.

Finally, someone has been to see them. We all want news. Darrell is as proud as a dad could be; strong; okay. Simone is more fragile. Dawnisha has a strawberry birthmark on her forehead and a purple splash over her nose. Her left arm is three-fourths the normal length, with three fingers. Her right arm is only a small hand with three fingers at the shoulder. But—a hopeful "but" this time—everything else seems to be okay. The doctor predicted she'll do everything but throw a ball.

July—A Smucker gathering; Darrell and Simone are coming. We are all eager to see the baby. Eager, and apprehensive.

My first impulse, when I see Dawnisha, is to gasp. My second is to hold her and love her. She looks somehow long and narrow; she feels like she will slip out of my hands. I never realized before how a baby's arms make it look balanced, and how one naturally grasps a baby under the arms. Dawnisha opens her eyes and looks at me. I have never seen such eyes on a baby—calm, wise, aware. This baby will be fine, her eyes tell me.

The cousins take turns holding Jenny and Dawnisha. I can't help but compare these two babies, and I feel guilty for having a "perfect" baby, like I should take her out of the room so no one can compare the two.

Simone has so much piled on her at one time. The adjustments to a dependent new baby are difficult in the best of times. On top of that, nursing isn't going well; Dawnisha isn't gaining weight and doesn't sleep well. Simone had hoped to have her baby on a schedule; it's not working. Simone has a bad case of post-partum depression. And, of course, the baby is handicapped.

Why her and not me? I wonder, over and over. I was the one who took medication for the nausea. I, at least, had already been through the enormous adjustments to motherhood itself. Was I incapable of loving a handicapped child, so she was given to Simone and not to me? Or had I already learned the lessons Simone was supposed to learn through this?

Pondering this tangle of questions leads me nowhere, of course. With time, I am able to accept that this is how things are, how they were somehow meant to be. I have Jenny; she has Dawnisha—both miracles, both gifts, both loved.

August—Simone switches to formula and gives up on breastfeeding. She abandons her schedule. Dawnisha begins to gain weight. Everyone is happier.

Fall—Jenny can smile, babble, reach, grab. She learns to sit up, then crawl. Dawnisha is also acquiring skills, with her own unique twist. She reaches with the longer of her arms and pinches things with her fingers. She learns to sit up, kick her legs, and swivel in circles on the floor. When she's happy, her grin radiates from her entire face.

At church one Sunday, Jenny is too noisy to remain in the service. I take her to the foyer and set her on the floor to play. Darrell soon joins me with Dawnisha and sets her beside Jenny. Dawnisha drops her pacifier. I see her looking at it, lying on the floor in front of her. She swivels one way, then the other, and can't reach it. *Please get it,* I think. *Please find a way.* Dawnisha leans forward and scoops up the pacifier with her mouth. I'm ecstatic. Behind the pacifier, I see Dawnisha's delighted grin.

I compare Dawnisha's progress with Jenny's, and am troubled when Dawnisha lags behind. When I examine my attitudes, I don't like what I see. Why do I place so much value on accomplishment and beauty? Why can't I celebrate each child's uniqueness?

July—Simone and I sit in my front yard under the oak tree. I'm having a yard sale; she's helping me out. We watch Jenny and Dawnisha play, rescue them occasionally, scoop them up to hug them. Simone talks about mothering a handicapped child. "I'm no longer uncomfortable when I meet a person in a wheelchair," she says. "I go up to them and talk. Having a child like Dawnisha opens up a whole new world. I've met the most wonderful people."

We sit in the shade and wait for customers.

"What's been the hardest thing?" I ask her.

"It's the people who pity me!" Simone says emphatically. "They come by, pat my shoulder, 'Oh, bless you, bless you.' I want to ask them, 'Why do you feel sorry for me? *Why?*'"

We leave her question hanging in midair, unanswered. I think of a conversation I had recently with a woman whose son has cerebral palsy.

"I've decided," she said, "that my son isn't the one with the problem. He is fine. It's the rest of us who have the problem."

A car pulls in the driveway and a young woman jumps out and asks how to get to Monroe. I give her directions and she hops back in the car. Simone looks at me, stunned. "Did you see that? She had only two fingers on her hand! I'm going to talk to her!"

Simone sprints off after the car. Two minutes later, she is back. She has exchanged phone numbers with the young woman and is having her over for dinner soon.

Twenty feet away, Jenny and Dawnisha sit in a patch of sunshine and help each other pull apart a stack of books, carefully, one by one. Taking turns, it seems.

Dealing
With Matt

*T*hings haven't been easy lately with a teenager in the house—conflicts flare up at odd moments over the oddest of issues. Also, we keep running out of food, which is why Matt, age 14, and I are in the van, headed to WinCo on a Saturday night.

Not long ago, Matt found an article in *Reader's Digest* that he thought I should read. It was titled "What Moms Need To Know About Sons" and encouraged mothers to make deals with their boys. I've been trying, but with Matt's quick logic, I usually find myself caught in a fog of reasoning that ends us up far away from my intended goal. When he was a toddler, I used to go to bed and cry because I was sure he was going to end up in prison. Now I go to bed and worry that he'll be a slick lawyer, keeping criminals out of prison on technicalities.

But tonight I've struck a deal that works: "You eat so much, you help me get groceries. Deal?" Deal.

At a garage sale recently I found a book that I thought might help us. It's called *But You Don't Understand*. Before I had a chance to read it, Matt started reading it and thought it was just what his parents needed. My husband, in a moment of dubious generosity, told Matt to indicate which passages he wanted his parents to note especially. So as we head down the long straight stretch of Highway 99, Matt is beside me frowning over the book, enormous left shoe hooked over bony right knee, highlighting in yellow the passages meant for his dad and underlining in black the things I need to hear. The page he's on now is evidently meant for both of us; it looks like the back of some giant mutant bumblebee.

I ask him bravely what it is right there that I need to hear.

"This talks about listening to your teenager," he says offhandedly, and keeps on underlining.

I am stunned. He thinks I don't listen to him? I think back over the years, all the times I put down a book to listen to a mind-numbing play-by-play of his soccer game at school. And what about the thousands of questions I've answered? Doesn't that count for anything? When he was 3, I decided to count, and in one day he asked—and I answered—115 "why" questions.

"So you think I don't listen to you?" I whimper.

He is matter-of-fact: "You don't listen to me when I try to tell you something you should change."

So that's it—how dare he? I flare up in self-defense, then realize just as quickly that that's exactly what he's talking about. So I shrivel up, chastened, and say, "Oh."

We pull into the WinCo parking lot, get out, and find a cart. He loved to ride in the cart when he was little. Later he liked to grab the handle when I wasn't looking, set his feet on the bar at the bottom, and ride off down the cereal aisle like Blackfinger Wolf in *The Great Supermarket Mystery*. I consider asking if he wants to ride in the cart, just as a joke, but decide not to. I tell him this, so he knows I'm catching on.

He says, "It's a good thing you didn't. That book says that you shouldn't treat your teen like a baby."

While I compare prices on diapers, he takes off for the bulk foods and weighs out bags of jawbreakers and bubble gum. A bundle of paradoxes, he wastes his money on junk food but economizes by buying it in bulk. And he is endlessly patient with his baby sister but got revenge on the little cousin that pelted him with a green walnut. He takes meticulous care of his pets' cages but lets his bedroom look disastrous. Part little boy, part grown-up, he keeps me guessing.

We stroll down the laundry aisle, and suddenly I spot it: "Zout!" I exclaim. "Yes! I've been looking everywhere for Zout! This is absolutely the *best* stain remover. I'm getting two!"

Matt taps me gently on the shoulder. "Uh, Mom? That book I'm reading says you shouldn't embarrass your teenager by making a scene in public."

He calls this making a scene in public? I wish he could remember the time he begged for a pack of gum and screamed so loudly that we got dirty looks from all over the store. Or the time we got on a plane and he wailed, "But I don't wanna go on the big airplane" over and over. We had to deal not only with him but with the advice of a dozen well-meaning strangers who were as desperate as we were to turn off this flood of noise.

In the cereal aisle, I bypass the boxes and head for the big cart-filling gunny sacks of Toasty-O's and Marshmallow Mateys. I had heard that teenage boys eat a lot, but I still wasn't prepared when Matt hit a growth spurt at 13. His favorite breakfast consists of a huge bowl of cereal followed by four pieces of toast slathered with peanut butter and jam. Speaking of peanut butter, we pick up a four-pound barrel of it at the end of the aisle. If we're lucky, it will last for two weeks.

On the way home, Matt is quiet and the book stays, unopened, on the dashboard. I treasure these moments with him, undistracted by younger siblings, just the two of us. I ask him what animals he'd like to get.

"Well, of course, I always want a milk snake, but I don't suppose you'd let me."

"That's right."

"But you've kind of gotten to where you think my lizards are cute, right?"

I nod.

"Well, I have this plan. I figure if you've gotten used to anoles, then next I can get long-tailed lizards until you get used to those, then I'll get legless lizards, and then I'll get a snake and you won't mind."

I snort. "You'll have to do better at keeping your animals contained if you ever want a snake. I don't appreciate getting woken up at 5 in the morning by a hamster tapping on my head."

He chuckles. "Oh, *Mom*, hamsters are different. I wouldn't let a snake out of my room, okay?"

We slow down to drive through Junction City.

"Would you mind if I got a centipede?" he asks.

I picture a harmless three-inch worm and am about to tell him it would be fine. However, I haven't lived with him for 14 years for nothing. "What kind of a centipede are we talking, here?"

When the subject is animals, he always sounds like he's reading out of a book. "It's called a Giant Peruvian Centipede and on average it's about 17 inches long." (I picture a 17-inch centipede on my pillow at 5 a.m.) "But it has a bite that's mildly poisonous, and we do have a baby in the house, so I would settle for a millipede that's 7 inches long."

I sigh. I'm happy to see this concern for his sister, but still, he would "settle for a millipede"? Who said we were making a deal here?

Ordinary Days

The house is dark when we get home. Matt helps me carry in groceries and says he's going to bed. I remind him to brush his teeth. (We have a deal—he'll take better care of his teeth and I'll consider Madagascar hissing cockroaches.) "Good night," I say. "Thanks for your help. I love you."

"Uh-huh," he says, his mouth full of Kit Kats. He heads upstairs, placing his enormous tennis shoes cautiously on each step—his baby sister and the lizards are sleeping, you know. He'd hate to wake them up.

Later, I pick up *But You Don't Understand*, flip to an underlined page, and begin to read. "Mutual Respect" is underlined and highlighted. Sounds like a deal to me.

Seasons

Harvest

hen I first came to Oregon, I thought I knew a lot about farming.

After all, I had driven pickup loads of pigs to the sale barn and skipped school to drive a Farmall M tractor all day. And I could drive by a farm and tell with one sniff if they raised pigs, cows, or chickens there.

I knew quite a bit about Minnesota farming, I guess, but I didn't know anything about Oregon farming.

In the Willamette Valley, I found myself surrounded by the grass fields between Halsey and Harrisburg. I was fascinated by them—"Once a farmer, always a farmer"—but I found the local farming a strange, new world.

I had always thought that all respectable fields sprouted in the spring, grew all summer, and turned brown after the first frost in the fall. Then, of course, they remained frozen all winter. Oregon fields were harvested in midsummer and turned green again in the fall, then they stayed green all winter. Rain and green grass in January—it was like seeing the sun rise in the west.

Oregon farmers also had a vocabulary all their own—ryegrass, fescue, orchardgrass. (I imagined a newspaper headline—"Rescue in the Fescue.") Instead of taking their seed to an elevator in town, it seemed that every other farmer had a "warehouse" of his own. This was not only a storage building, I found out; it was also a place to clean and bag the grass seed.

In Oregon, teenage girls drove enormous John Deere combines during harvest. Where I came from, combines were driven by beefy men in Pioneer seed-corn caps. Then, after harvest, the Oregon farmers deliberately set their fields on fire. Amazing.

"You need to stay around for harvest," people kept telling me that first winter. They said the word like it was special, weighted—*"Harvest."* So, after my teaching job was finished, I found short-term work and followed their advice. That summer I was an observer. In recent years I have become a participant, as my husband Paul first managed and then bought his dad's warehouse.

Harvest, I've learned, is much more than bringing in the crop. For the farming community, it's the focal point of the year. Harvest implies the ambiance of warm summer days, of family history, of the land. Harvest is a hurricane, predicted and anticipated, that blows in and sweeps an entire community into the storm.

For farmers, the seasonal cycle converges at the end of June. Their entire livelihood depends on this narrow window of just a few days, when the seed is ripe for cutting. Cut too soon, the seeds are not filled out well. Too late, and they shatter easily and fall to the ground. In the months leading up to June, as the grass grows taller and forms heads, cousin Trish's husband, Richard, starts having nightmares: his neighbor is already out cutting. Richard panics and then wakes up, startled, relieved to know it's only a dream.

The combines start whining into the fields about a week after the grass is cut. From mid-morning, when the dew dries, until the dew forms again after dark, they circle the fields, eating up the neat windrows and spitting a stream of seed into the tank behind the driver. When the tank is full, a truck pulls alongside the combine. A long arm, like the head and neck of a dinosaur, swivels out from the combine and coughs the seed into the bed of the truck. From there the seed is taken to a warehouse.

Our warehouse was built by Paul's grandfather, Orval Smucker, who was one of the many farmers after World War II who grew grass seed and built a warehouse to process it themselves. He built it several hundred yards away from his house, across Muddy Creek, which meanders by in a U shape.

The end of June, with its warm, sunny days after months of rain, matures the crop to perfection. It also lures children to the creek. Generations of Smucker children have spent their summer afternoons playing in the water. Little children play in the ford, skittering out of the way when a combine comes by to cross where the creek is shallowest. While their dads sweat in the heat and dust of the warehouse or the fields, the medium-sized cousins float on inner tubes near the bridge, and the biggest kids swim down by the "deep hole."

This summer, our 14-year-old son Matthew has graduated from swimming in the creek to working in the warehouse for four hours a day. Before his first shift, I look at Matthew's skinny, freckled arms and try to imagine them lifting 50-pound sacks.

"Paul, are you sure he's ready for this?" I ask.

Paul is sure. He knows, better than I do, this rite of passage. He and dozens of others in the family and the neighborhood were once skinny, freckled teenagers who went from playing in the creek to that first real job—sacking seed in the warehouse or working in the fields.

At the warehouse, Matthew works on the bottom floor of a tall building that vibrates and rumbles as the seed passes through the cleaners—a series of fans and screens. This removes the weed seeds and chaff, and the pure seed falls into a hopper. Matthew slips a bag onto a weighing machine at the end of the hopper, and the bag fills with 50 pounds of seed. Some types of bags close by themselves. Other bags are sewn shut with a portable sewing device dangling from the ceiling. He then stacks the bag onto a pallet and repeats this process up to 80 times an hour. The pallets of seed are stacked in another part of the warehouse until they are sold and shipped.

Amy is 12. She hopes in a couple of years to get a job driving a combine. Again, I can hardly imagine it—this petite, feminine child handling such a behemoth of a machine. Her aunts will no doubt assure me that she will do fine. I vividly remember Paul's sisters Rosie and Barb stumbling in the door at 10 on summer evenings after a day on the combine. Invariably they were exhausted and covered with dust. Despite the dust, I saw a sense of pride. They had handled the behemoth all day, done a good job, earned some money. And when the time comes, I won't deny Amy the same sense of accomplishment.

Everyone approaches harvest a bit differently, but they share a commitment to getting the job done. No one takes a vacation now, and anything optional is postponed. Paul has the cleaners running 24 hours a day during July and August. He leaves the house early in the morning and works at the warehouse for up to 14 hours a day. Sometimes he gets up in the middle of the night to repair a cleaner that breaks down.

One farmer we know works at night to cut the grass—the seed doesn't shatter as much at night, he says. Another one is up at 6 a.m. to haul screenings—warehouse byproducts—before he starts combining at 10. Some people work seven days a week, like Roy, who drives seed to our warehouse.

He works all day, every day, for two months. Paul, on the other hand, takes Sundays off, and we all go to church, where sunburned farmers nod off during the sermon.

Harvest always disrupts our family's routine, and it falls on me to keep everything running smoothly behind the scenes. I fit meals around warehouse schedules, put the children to bed at night by myself, and wash piles of dirty laundry, first emptying handfuls of grass seed from Paul's and Matthew's pockets.

Most of my friends are in the same situation. Margaret's husband hires a crew of up to 10, most of them teenagers, every summer. Margaret goes from cooking for two to driving out to the fields every evening to feed 10 or 15 people a hot meal from the back of her pickup truck. In addition, she becomes a mom to the five teenagers who stay at their house—cooking for them, doing their laundry, and reminding them to use deodorant. Trish leaves her toddler with her mother-in-law and drives a combine for two weeks. Other women drive trucks from the field to the warehouse, or spend hours on the road, driving to town for parts for machinery that breaks down.

This, too, is how it has always been. I remember how, when we were first married, I watched my mother-in-law with a sense of awe. It wasn't possible to get any busier than this, I was sure, as I watched her flying in a dozen directions to take care of her family during harvest. She'd prepare a huge, hot meal at noon for anyone who happened to be in the house. Then she'd fill plates and deliver them to anyone who wasn't at home—Rosie on her combine, Barb on hers, a husband and son at the warehouse.

After lunch, the "night guy," who worked the night shift at the warehouse and boarded with my in-laws, would wake up and stumble downstairs. Anne would scurry around the kitchen to fix him bacon and eggs. I suggested once that she save herself some work and let the night guy eat whatever she had made for lunch. Anne wouldn't hear of it. Everyone deserves a proper breakfast when they wake up, she said. This was Harvest, after all, and this was her calling—to keep everyone fed and cared for.

Harvest is an exciting time, busy, suspenseful. But underneath is an awareness of danger. A spark from a combine can quickly ignite a dry field, bringing fire trucks wailing down the back roads. Paul's cousin Don lost both of his feet when they were caught in a combine header almost 30 years ago. Field burning, once popular but now done less often, has its own dangers. Paul's sister burned her legs one summer when she was igniting the straw from the back of a pickup truck. A brother-in-law was caught in a field fire when the wind shifted. He survived, but with scars.

Many farmers mourn the demise of field burning. They now have to find new ways to get rid of the straw and deal with insects and disease. While the cycle of the seasons remains the same year after year, change is inevitable.

"In my opinion, farming has changed more in the last five or 10 years than it did in the previous 25," says Richard Baker, a local farmer. "The way the seed is marketed, the way we treat disease, everything. And I think it will keep changing just as fast."

Farming may change, but a farmer once is a farmer always. Paul's grandpa Orval is now 94 years old. His awareness is gradually dimming, but even in the last few years it is obvious that he is a farmer at heart.

"That ryegrass is about ready for cuttin,'" he'd shout at me in his raspy voice as I drove him to my house.

Every time he saw me sewing he would tell me about an accident at the warehouse one harvest.

"You ever get'cher finger in that sewing machine?" he'd shout. "I had a guy at the warehouse one time was sacking seed, and when he sewed up the sack he sewed right through his thumb! When I got there, there was a whole bunch of guys around him tryin' to pick this string out of his thumb real careful. Well, I just went up to 'im and took hold of that string and gave it a good yank and out it come! No need to be so careful with it!"

He always chuckled, and I always shuddered in sympathy for that poor warehouse worker. Grandpa repeated and embellished this story a number of times—one version even had the guy sewing his lower lip to the sack. Later I learned that, in reality, the worker had been taken to the doctor to have the string removed from his thumb.

Orval is in a nursing home in Eugene, and his grandson now owns the warehouse. A new young man is sacking seed, and new ways of farming are blowing into the Valley. But, once again, it's July and farmers anxiously watch the weather, children play in the creek, and the grass lies piled in neat windrows, waiting to be harvested.

As one of my favorite Bible verses promises—"As long as the earth endures, seedtime and harvest, cold and heat, summer and winter, day and night will never cease."

Daffodils in Spring

Someone asked me not long ago if I prefer the climate here in Oregon or in Minnesota, where I grew up.

"I like both," I said. And then, growing nostalgic, I added, "But I really miss the snow."

In Minnesota, the weather was dramatic. Terrible thunderstorms in summer were followed by crisp fall mornings that turned everything brown. The first real snowfall changed the landscape, overnight, from a dull brown to a gleaming white. Fierce blizzards blew in, shut everything down, and then sculpted a dazzling landscape of sharp-edged, curving drifts. And in spring, the landscape changed again, from white, to a muddy brown, to a sudden green.

When I first came to Oregon, I researched the climate by looking on a map. It looked like I would be living just as far north as I was in Minnesota, so I concluded that the climate would be pretty much the same. That fall, in Oregon, I kept waiting for the cold weather, for snow, for winter. Instead, each chilly, rainy day was followed by another. I asked my roommate when the fields would start turning brown. She replied that they stayed green all winter, and I thought she must be crazy. I asked her where I should plug in my car at night when it got cold, and she thought I was crazy.

Christmas came—still no snow. Surely it was illegal to have Christmas with rain and green grass outside. The weeks and the weather dragged on, with none of the drama of a good thunderstorm or blizzard, only this constant, dripping, disgusting, sloppy, wet rain. I thought it was awful.

I admit, there were also a few disadvantages to a Minnesota winter: slippery roads, shoveling snow, and February. We called it the February blues, this malaise that settled in when Christmas was long gone, the cold was unrelenting, and it seemed that spring would never come. The snow, piled beside streets and sidewalks, was gray and dirty. We were all tired of starting cars on cold mornings and wearing parkas and boots. With this fatigue came a dullness, a lack of motivation. Who could get inspired to try something new when the world was locked in by cold and we were focused on surviving, on waiting for spring?

I had a touch of the February blues my first winter in Oregon—I was sick and tired of dull gray skies and unrelenting rain. Then, one afternoon when the rain let up for a little while, a friend from next door asked me to go on a bike ride with her. I was hunkered down by the electric heater, as I recall, trying to solve my Rubik's cube, but I agreed to leave my comfortable spot and go with her. We headed down the country roads, past wet, mossy trees, wet grass in the ditches, wet fields, and wet blackberry bushes.

Suddenly, I spotted something astonishing: daffodils. Right there, growing in a field beside the road, were dozens of green clumps, bursting with hundreds of daffodils.

"What are they doing there?" I asked my friend. "Who planted them?"

She shrugged. "I don't know. They just grow there."

I couldn't believe it—daffodils. Not coaxed carefully out of a flower bed in May, but popping, all on their own, out of a mint field in February. Such lavish extravagance. It was like finding pearls in a sack of potatoes. I was still waiting for winter, and here in front of me were hundreds of daffodils like pert little girls in ruffly sunbonnets.

I had a new perspective after that. Winter in Oregon might be dripping and dull, but, before it was over, long before spring, it treated me to an abundance of flowers.

The February blues crept up on me again this year, even though there was less rain than usual. I had too many pounds left over from Christmas. The children ignored too many of my requests, and I was letting too many people take advantage of me. Things needed to change, and I needed motivation to change them.

My mother-in-law's daffodils were always the first ones in the neighborhood to bloom. When she and her husband moved out of their house, and we moved in, I wondered if the daffodils would bloom for me like they did for her. By the end of January, a row of bushy green clumps of leaves grew under the grape arbor. Soon, buds formed.

I bought a jump rope and began using it, stumbling over the rope and gasping for breath. One weekend, I went to a church women's retreat at the coast, finding new strength in walks on the beach, talks with other women, and ideas from the guest speaker.

"Don't yell or nag at your children," she told us. "Say the child's name, wait until he looks at you, and then give a command in a quiet voice."

When I came home, the house was clean and a bouquet of daffodils stood on the kitchen table. "I picked them," my daughter beamed. "Did you know they're blooming?"

No, I hadn't known, and found a childish delight in knowing that I, like my mother-in-law, could grow the first daffodils in the neighborhood.

In the next weeks, as more and more daffodils bloomed and bouquets dotted the house, I worked my way up from a hundred rope-jumps a day, to two hundred, to three. I tried the retreat speaker's advice with my children and found that such a simple thing made an amazing difference. I found the courage to say "No" to unreasonable expectations—once, then again.

While I still get nostalgic for winter in Minnesota, with glittering snowdrifts under a blue sky, I've decided that I love February in Oregon, where daffodils bloom staunchly in the rain, and change seems possible—not in dramatic leaps, but one, small, confident step at a time.

Summer Vacation

I paid 10 cents to see the performance, and it is easily worth the money.

Three days into summer vacation, my 11-year-old daughter Emily and her cousin Stephanie have formed Ladybug Enterprises. This is their first business venture, a play called "Let Sisterly Love Continue" which, since three of us came to watch, will net them exactly 30 cents.

Having handed over my red ticket, I perch on a tiny folding chair in my children's playhouse and watch as the girls pretend to be two sisters, "Sara" and "Jo," who can't get along.

The play involves an awful lot of costume changes and exaggerated arguing, along with occasional suffocating squirts of garage-sale perfume and hissed reminders—"No, Stephie! You don't say that now! Remember?"

Proceeding with dreamlike slowness, the plot moves from planning a party, to shopping for the party, to—finally—the party.

"Did you remember to invite Jason Fife?" "Sara" asks "Jo."

Jason Fife? Ah, yes, the Ducks' quarterback. I must be dreaming. "Sara" rushes to the door to let him in, and there is 8-year-old Ben, his dad's old suit coat hanging to his knees, an ominous lump bulging under his T-shirt, high on his chest.

"Jason" swaggers into the room and immediately eats an enormous amount of hors d'oeuvres, to the girls' dismay. He also keeps hitching up the lump, which wants to slide to his stomach. I see through the neck of his T-shirt that it's his sisters' old rag doll.

Ben's role is obviously a generous attempt by the girls to involve him in the action. The only thing he does to advance the plot is increase the sisters' rivalry when he pays more attention to "Jo" than "Sara."

The performance eventually ends with the "sisters" apologizing and mending their relationship, wild applause from the audience, and Ben shedding his costume with a sigh of relief.

"Why the doll?" I ask Ben. He shrugs. "To look, you know, buff."

Emily adds, "We thought it would look more realistic on his shoulders, but we couldn't get it to stay there."

This is why I like summer vacation.

Math and science are good things, of course, and I'm grateful that my children can get an education in a school that reinforces our religious beliefs—with their dad, no less, as the principal. But I am convinced that while subjects and schedules nourish a child's mind and self-discipline, something in his spirit goes hungry.

This year, as always, the last weeks of school were a flurry of finishing—tests, the yearbook, and preparations for the end-of-year program. In contrast, the sun shone warm on the basketball court, and the poppies beside Highway 228 waved serenely as we drove home from school.

On that last Friday, folders and battered pencil cases were hauled home in grocery sacks, and the program proceeded without a ripple.

And then, officially, it was summer, a block of time so vast that, to a child, it might as well be forever. September is a dim shore on the other side of the ocean as they launch out from May, a vague ending to a vast sea of opportunity.

For children, the best thing about summer is that, at last, there's time. No rush to be out the door by 8 a.m. No precious evenings swallowed by homework. There's time to not only imagine, but to test their ideas, modify them, and try something new. There's enough time to plan a treehouse for the walnut tree or a raft for the creek, and enough time to build it, play in it with the cousins, remodel it, and have it turn into a fort, a ship, or a dozen other things by the end of the summer.

Ladybug Enterprises has already considered a dozen money-making schemes, usually over the phone. The play, of course, was a success. Other ideas were rejected.

"Hello, Stephie? I don't think I can get Dad to build us a little craft shop after all."

And others are still being tested. "Stephie? I have an idea. Maybe we can bake cookies and put them at the warehouse to sell after harvest starts. And I planted a bunch of marigolds in my garden. Maybe we can make bouquets and sell them."

Summer gives children a chance to work with their hands— to plant corn in freshly-tilled dirt, to hoe the weeds, eventually to harvest and eat the corn. Or to hang heavy, wet towels on the clothesline and bring them in hours later, warm with sunshine and smelling of summer. For 16-year-old Matt, sacking 50-pound bags of grass seed all summer provides an entirely different sense of satisfaction than finishing a research paper.

For me, summer has always been a time of transition, a time to look back and evaluate, and to look ahead and plan. The change from the old year to the new on January 1 has always seemed much too abrupt. Thanks to a teacher dad, my own school years, a teacher husband, and my children, I have been able to work with the rhythms of the school year for most of my life, easing out of the old year and into the new with a complete change of schedule and activities in between.

Eventually, of course, I'll receive a back-to-school flyer and I'll look at the calendar and count, shocked to realize that only a few weeks of summer remain. I will suddenly grow tired of sticky orange Kool-Aid spots on the kitchen floor, and Ben will flop on the couch and moan, "I'm bored!"

Soon, crisp new school uniforms will hang in the closets, the house will seem full of restless children, and a strict schedule will sound strangely appealing.

Then, tanned, refreshed, and nostalgic, my children will rush out the door on a September morning. Savoring the peace and quiet, I will untangle the last wet, wadded swimsuit in the laundry room and reflect gratefully on summer vacation, when anything is possible, and for a dime I can see my son turned into a quarterback, buff and hungry.

"Hunting" Season

The children are easy to rouse on this Friday morning, bouncing out of bed with a sense of anticipation. "I wanna go to the godge sale," my 2-year-old Jenny squeaks from her crib. I've trained her well.

Garage saling involves many things: family bonding, adventure, and thrift. But primarily, like a New Guinean tribal ritual, this is all about "The Hunt." Equipment, strategy, and prey. Success or disappointment.

While the children eat breakfast in the early-morning chill, I gather my supplies. My hunting equipment comes not from Cabela's but from garage sales: wallet, tote bag, toys, and snack containers.

I scan the garage-sale page in the classifieds and choose the terrain: the Ferry Street Bridge section. Smugly, I pull out my cleverest hunting tool, designed to give me an edge over all the amateurs out there. It's a map I cut from the phone book and then laminated. I call out the name of a street—"Brewer!" and my daughter Amy finds it in the index from the phone book— "F-11!" I mark the street with a washable marker, and soon the map is dotted with little red lines.

Then, with a sense of urgency, we grab the bags and water bottles and pile into the car. Buckle the baby, check the supplies, and, as always, take a few seconds to pray. "Dear God, please watch over us today, and help us find a few bargains."

It's 8:15 already. Someone else is there ahead of me, I'm sure, loading up the toddler bed I want, picking through the fabric, taking the white Corelle dishes. As my Aunt Vina used to say, rushing toward Iowa City, "We need to hurry before all the hoarders get there!"

Our first stop is at Harry's Berries, south of Coburg, only now the fruit stand is full of crocheted doilies and home-school books instead of strawberries. Amy tugs on my sleeve and says she wants to show me something. It's a piece of luggage, on wheels, just what we've been looking for. A Samsonite, and only a dollar! There must be a catch. Wheels are good, handles attached. There it is—the zipper is torn at one corner.

This is the great garage-sale gamble. If I can fix it, it'll be the best bargain of the day. If I can't, it'll be a dollar wasted and a big piece of junk on my hands. I examine it further.

"You know, if I'd stitch it up right there, the zipper couldn't go past that bad spot, but I could still use it without that little bit of zipper at the end." Verdict: I'll take it.

Mrs. Garage Sale, a delightful elderly woman, is eager to talk. She recently got married, she tells me, and her husband makes the most wonderful things out of wood, including this lovely bench. I agree, it really is a beautiful bench, and just what I want to put along one side of our kitchen table. But for $25? New things, however fairly they may be priced, seem absurdly expensive at garage sales. Plus, I'm not sure the bench is long enough. Verdict: No.

Most of us garage salers have severe Someone-Could-Use-This syndrome. We give our moms copies of cookbooks they already own and buy our nieces clothes that are the wrong size and don't match anything in their closets. Cell phones, thankfully, are changing all that. I whip out mine and call my friend Simone.

"You know that book you told me I should check out of the Harrisburg library? *Lord Foulgrin's Letters*? I'm at a garage sale and they have a copy of it here. Three dollars." Yes, she'd love to have it, but I'm supposed to read it first. Deal.

Ordinary Days

South on Coburg Road, right on Crescent. Garage sale signs pop out of the trees, luring us down side streets. There are two kinds of garage sales, my husband says: the kind where people are trying to get rid of stuff, announced by hand-lettered Magic Marker on cardboard. And the kind where people are trying to make money, indicated by carefully stenciled letters on wood. Not that there's anything wrong with making money, but we brake for cardboard.

Sandals, wedding decorations, Yosemite souvenirs. The thing about being poor in America, my brother says, is that you can live so well off wealthier people's cast-offs. I find a children's book for Jenny—hardcover, like new, beautiful watercolor pictures of farm animals. New price: $15.99. I pay 25 cents.

We work our way southwest: Brewer, Lemming, Goodpasture Island. High chairs, 8-track tapes, paperback romances. A rack of blouses, just my style and colors, but double my size. Jenny finds chairs to sit on, the older girls rummage in "free" boxes, and 8-year-old Ben, already bored, stays in the car and reads.

Amy and Emily discover a dress and beg me to buy it. "Wouldn't this be adorable on Jenny?" It's worth a dollar to find something the three of us agree on. I buy it.

Fishing poles, orange stuffed chairs, coffee pots. I briefly consider an electric knife, still in the box, as a potential gift. Yes, I confess: I've given garage-sale items as gifts, although I've never experienced what a friend of mine did. She bought a slightly-used Crock Pot, along with the box, at a garage sale, then polished it up and gave it as a wedding gift. Later the bride told her, "We got quite a few Crock Pots at our wedding, so I took yours to Kmart and exchanged it for something else. I hope you don't mind."

Amy wants me to buy her a flower-shaped key chain that costs 50 cents. Too much, I think.

"But, Mom, it's all sparkly, and see, it's a little picture frame, too."

Should I offer less? Dickering at garage sales is allowed, even encouraged. My husband almost always offers less than the posted price, just to see what happens. I dicker only if I feel the marked price is too high. Just as I am ready to do so, the owner offers to reduce the price to 20 cents. I take it.

By 10, we're all hungry, the children are ready to call it a day, and Jenny is whining in her car seat. Reluctantly, I agree, as I still need to get groceries and want to be home by 11. Ben hands out snacks as we head for WinCo.

Garage sale signs flutter from stop signs, beckoning me.

"HUGE SALE."

"MULTI-FAMILY."

All right, just one more.

This one turns out to be an estate sale, full of expensive old things I don't want, which serves me right. We leave, and the signs continue.

Look! Right here! Please? It'll only take a minute! Just one more!

Resolutely, I set my face toward WinCo and pass them by.

At home, we unload the car and eat lunch, weary hunters home from the hill, sailors home from the sea. I hold Jenny on my lap and we read her new book, where the cow, the pigs, and the chickens all go to sleep. Soon, she joins them.

"Hunting" season will be over when the rains begin. In a few weeks, while the weather holds, I'll catch a whiff of bargains in the wind, and we'll set out again on a chilly Saturday morning. Just once more.

Autumn Harvest

fter years of hit-or-miss breakfasts, my husband Paul and I decided three years ago to start getting everyone up for a sit-down family breakfast every morning. We drew up a chart, and each of us was responsible for setting the table and making breakfast one morning of the week.

For a long time, Paul and I were the only ones who put any effort into our breakfasts, his specialty being pancakes, and mine, breakfast burritos. The children, on their mornings, all served the same easy cold cereal and toast. We decided not to push the issue, hoping that eventually maturity and initiative would blossom and the children would try something more complicated. But the cereal and toast continued, week after week, month after month.

Last week, however, I was awakened at six one morning by clattering in the kitchen. I found Amy, age 13, dressed and alert, stirring up a batch of muffins for our breakfast. She found a recipe in an American Girl cookbook and decided to try it, she said. A few days later, as 11-year-old Emily headed upstairs to bed one evening, I heard her asking Paul to get her up early so he could teach her how to make blueberry pancakes.

For me, these two incidents were like finding the first ripe tomato hidden in the vines—a rich reward for a summer of waiting and work.

At this time of year, signs of fall are all around. When I park under the oak tree, I often am startled by a loud bang on top of the car, the sound far larger than the acorn that caused it.

Across the driveway, walnuts lie scattered on the grass like Lego blocks on a bedroom carpet. The maples arching across Powerline Road drip wet, yellow leaves on my windshield as I drive underneath.

It's the season of ripening, harvesting, and gathering in.

The grapevines south of the house were stripped weeks ago. The apples from our trees are stored in grass-seed sacks in the back porch or turned to applesauce. In the garden, the beans are tilled under and the cornstalks chopped down and hauled away. Fat jars of green beans sit placidly on my shelves, and the corn is tucked away in the freezer, stiff and yellow in Ziploc bags. I canned the last of the tomatoes not long ago, listening for that satisfying little "ping!" as the last jar sealed.

Summer is the season of diligence: weeding, watering, and watching for bugs. Now, I'm leaving the garden to marinate in mud until next May. All summer, I hovered over the potted plants, pinching here, coaxing there. In the fall, I compost the leftover petunias and stack the flowerpots in the back porch. The walnuts are drying in old pillowcases by the furnace. At our grass-seed warehouse, the summer's crop is cleaned and bagged, and Paul is planning projects around the house—insulating under the floor and installing the new range hood in the kitchen. It's time to unpack my wool sweaters, plan sewing projects, and watch the leaves on the snowball bush turn red.

Nature and the calendar tell me it's fall, but in the timeline of our lives, our family is only in mid-summer.

Our five children range in age from 2 to 15, and this is our season of hard work, constant activity, and endless vigilance. The laundry hampers always seem to be full, triple batches of cookies disappear magically, and the kitchen floor seldom stays clean for more than half an hour. Our schedules are full

Ordinary Days

of school and church activities, doctor and dentist appointments, piano lessons and drivers'-ed classes. I am constantly vigilant: alert, monitoring, averting disaster. Does Jenny have an earache? Is Amy extra quiet, or is it just my imagination? Ben needs new jeans for school, Amy needs new contact lenses, and Emily needs a birthday gift for her friend's party. I never know when I'll find 2-year-old Jenny snipping my grocery coupons into little pieces, or when Matt's latest scientific experiment will dim all the lights in the house.

"Enjoy these years," older women tell me, and I do. I'm past the teenage agonies of wondering what to do with my life, and I treasure this time of knowing exactly what I'm supposed to be doing. Raising my family is, I believe, the most important work I'll ever do. At this stage I am never bored, constantly entertained, and seldom alone or lonely.

Yet, in this summer of my life, I watch for signs of fall. For our family, it's still a long way off.

"Do you realize," my son asked me last year, "that you're going to have at least one teenager in the house for the next 18 years?"

My husband's aunt, I'm told, can stitch a quilt in a week. "She likes to finish!" her sister tells me emphatically. "It's not that she enjoys the actual quilting that much. She just likes to finish!"

I, too, like to finish. I admit, I get such a thrill out of checking an item off my to-do list that I'll even write down something I already completed, just for the joy of checking it off.

As much as I enjoy this season of my life, I find that the most difficult thing about it is that it's so hard to finish anything—from sentences to grocery lists to painting a bedroom. My day's planned activities give way to a series of interruptions. My Saturday cleaning frenzies are never quite completed before it's time for supper and baths.

Of course, the biggest project of all takes the longest to finish—this enormous task of turning children into adults, responsible for their own decisions, capable of taking care of themselves.

I look forward to autumn. I anticipate a day when my children will apologize without being prompted and I'll hear one of them say, "Sure, you can sit in the front seat if you like." I look forward to seeing them consider our advice and then launch out on their own. Someday, I hope to complete this work, to feel finished, and to see the results of all these years of working and waiting.

This Thanksgiving, I am thankful for fall, this annual ritual of reaping and resting. I am thankful for my family and this season of our lives. And I give thanks for muffins and blueberry pancakes for breakfast, the taste of a fruitful autumn yet to come.

Christmas Memories

$\mathcal{M}$y mother always celebrated the holidays with huge Thanksgiving and Christmas dinners, homemade gifts, and cinnamon rolls for the mailman.

Best of all, she made candy and cookies: cut-out sugar cookies from the *Mennonite Community Cookbook*, fudge, "Divinity," and date pinwheels. We children helped with cutting out the sugar cookies and dipping peanut-butter balls in chocolate to make buckeyes.

Mom's Divinity was, as the name implies, almost divine. She would whip a bowl of egg whites, then stand at the stove and cook a sugary mixture to just the right temperature. She didn't have a candy thermometer, so she'd drop a dollop into a cup of cold water and expertly judge the temperature. Then the hot sugar syrup was folded into the egg whites and spread into a cake pan, where it cooled into a white, airy, irresistible treat.

For years, every November, I was struck by an urge to recreate these same memories for my children. It was this compulsion that made me say "yes" the time my friend Earl Baker offered us a turkey for Thanksgiving.

"You'll have to dress it yourself," he said. "Are you sure you know how?"

I had visions of chicken-butchering days on the farm—frosty mornings with steam rising from buckets of boiling water, Mom in her kerchief and old coat, and my sisters and me plucking the feathers. So I told Earl, "Sure, I know how to butcher a turkey."

That year on Thanksgiving, I kept glancing anxiously into the oven as the turkey turned a golden brown, and an ominous bulge by the neck grew larger and larger. Just before the guests arrived, I took the turkey out of the oven and inspected the bulge. It was the crop that I had forgotten to remove, and if I didn't cut carefully, I was going to have roasted grain all over the meat.

It may have been the same year that the children helped me make Christmas cookies. We began enthusiastically, but as the afternoon wore on, interest waned and tempers got shorter. By evening, every surface in the kitchen was sticky with icing and sprinkles, and stars and lopsided gingerbread men covered the counters.

My husband worked late that day so I had to clean up by myself, plus get all the children bathed and to bed. I kept turning up the thermostat and getting colder and colder.

Finally, I took my temperature and discovered I was coming down with the flu.

Then, 9-year-old Matt came slinking out of the bathroom. "Mom, I want to confess this before you discover it yourself: I made a tidal wave in the bathtub."

We mopped up the water and just as I collapsed into bed, Matt stuck his head in the door and told me that 2-year-old Ben wasn't sleeping, but was up and playing on the floor of their bedroom.

I survived that episode, of course, but I wondered if my children were going to remember only bumbling disasters at holidays. I had always assumed that my own warm memories of holiday traditions were a result of careful planning on

Mom's part, a determination to make sure we grew up with a generous stash of traditions and memories.

But I began to change my mind with a phone call from my sister a few years ago.

"Did you know that Mom doesn't remember making Divinity?" she demanded, consternation in her voice.

"What?" I asked.

"I'm serious. I called her for the recipe and she said, 'Divinity? Did I used to make Divinity?'"

There was silence on both ends of the line. *What did it mean? Alzheimer's? Dementia? Divinity was such a big part of Christmas,* we thought. *How could Mom possibly forget?* Yet her mind was still as sharp as ever in other areas, her letters interesting and articulate. It didn't make sense.

The next year, half afraid, I called Mom and asked for her buckeyes recipe.

"Buckeyes?" she said. "Hmmm . . . are those the ones Ervin Lyddie used to make?" (That would be my Uncle Ervin's wife, Lyddie, identified by her husband's name first in the Amish custom.)

"Ervin Lyddie?" I yelped. "No, Mom. *You* used to make them! Don't you remember?"

She didn't, at first, but then as I described them further she remembered that yes, maybe she had made them a time or two and had the recipe somewhere.

I made the buckeyes, dipping them in chocolate and wondering what to make of Mom's strange memory lapses.

Now, a year later, I've concluded that Mom forgot simply because it wasn't that important to her. Christmas candy was only one of a thousand details of her life that gradually changed as her children left home, and it wasn't important enough to remember 25 years later.

My sister once gave me a book called *Let's Make a Memory*. A collection of ideas for family activities, it encourages a goal of sending children into adulthood with a stockpile of good childhood memories.

This concept, I've decided, is born of the same era as self-esteem, quality time, and endlessly sharing one's feelings.

Mom had no use for such nebulous parenting. She believed in hard work, good food, fearing God, and having fun. In the process, our memories would take care of themselves.

Like the time I made Divinity—or tried to. I was probably 15, more into books than cooking, but Mom decided it was time I learned to make Divinity. She got out the recipe, gave me a few pointers, and went off to do something else. I separated the eggs, beat the whites, and cooked the sugary syrup.

Mom wasn't in the kitchen when I faced the next step, and the bare-bones recipe didn't tell me either. Was it syrup into egg whites or whites into syrup? Whites into syrup, I decided rashly, and when Mom came back into the kitchen I was staring, aghast, at the sick, crumbly mess I had just created, so different from Mom's fluffy Divinity.

She didn't get upset—that's what I remember best. She hated wasting food, and I often tried her patience. Yet, this time, when I did both, she was calm and reassuring.

"Hmmm," she said, poking dubiously at the gray mass, "Maybe Dad will eat it."

At our house, this was a polite way of saying, "I don't think the goats would touch it."

She was sure I'd remember next time. And I have never forgotten; it's syrup into egg whites. Even more, I haven't forgotten her response—warm and forgiving.

This year we want to make candy, give gifts, and eat a big Christmas dinner—with no memorable disasters, I hope.

Ultimately, though, Christmas is about love and redemption. If I focus on those gifts, the warm holiday memories are inevitable.

I think Mom knew all along that memories creep in when you're busy doing something else and when you least expect them, like a cat that slips in the front door when you open it to let your dinner guests come in.

And, like a contented cat, good memories curl up in a quiet corner and purr.

Relatives

An "Irrelevant" Generation

*T*he paper dolls always remind me of the afternoon last fall when I took Dad to the museum in Harrisburg. I find the dolls when I clean my daughters' room: chains of little girls, holding hands, all their braids connected to each other.

Mom had stayed with the children that afternoon, and when we came home, she was sitting on the couch with a narrow piece of folded paper in her hand. She cut a snip here, a careful curve there. As the children watched, fascinated, she slowly unfolded the paper and there was a row of little girls. She repeated the process and out came a chain of little boys in straw hats and bare feet. Before long, the children were folding and snipping under their grandma's direction. To me, it was confirmation that my parents' wisdom and skills were still relevant for my children, even though their lives are so different from Mom's and Dad's childhoods.

My parents had come from Minnesota by Amtrak to spend a week at our house. Mom is 80 years old; Dad is 84. Both grew up Amish, children of the Depression. In their younger years, they were ambitious, influential, and adventurous, pursuing travel and an education, unusual choices for the Amish. They married when Mom was 33 and Dad was 37, and had six children.

But now that my parents are older, it sometimes seems that the world has no use for people of their generation.

They are vast reservoirs of knowledge that no one is interested in. And modern society is a foreign country to my parents. It moves much too fast for them, and they are strangers in it, mystified by the customs, baffled by the language. They make brief forays away from home, then retreat gratefully back to their farm, where the phone still has a rotary dial, no one owns a credit card, and the chickens scratch and peck out by the barn. My parents are shocked and bewildered by modern lifestyles—all the wealth, the computers, the waste, the fast food, and the fractured families.

Mom and Dad's only source of world news is a weekly magazine. Mom reads about all the people making money on the stock market or the Internet. She sees them as vastly sophisticated but ignorant of the most basic skills.

"What if there was another Depression?" Mom often says, shaking her head. "How would people make it?"

She told me about the neighbor girl who came over to see if Mom and Dad wanted any kittens. "She had this skimpy little top on," Mom said, "with a ring in her belly button." Imagine.

Young people like that might drive their own cars and be experts with computers, but do they have any idea how to grow their own food, bake bread, butcher a chicken, or mend clothing? Mom doesn't think so. She worries about them.

I suggested one day that we all write an e-mail to my sister in Yemen. I got the computer ready and Mom sat down in front of it. Cautiously poking the right keys, she typed, "Dear Rebecca."

"Now what do I do?" she asked. "I want to go down to the next line."

Obviously, this wouldn't work. Instead, Mom and Dad wrote letters in longhand, and I typed them into the computer and announced that their letters would be at Becky's house within hours. Mom and Dad acted impressed, but their enthusiasm seemed a bit forced. *After all,* they probably thought, *a letter was a letter.* With one method, it would get there sooner and show up on a computer screen. With the other, it would take longer, but Becky could hold it in her hands and see Mom's firm handwriting with the spiky M's and Dad's perfect Palmer Method cursive. And who was to judge which was better?

We were shopping for a van during Mom and Dad's visit. On the way to Portland one day, Mom mended a pair of my son's jeans. Without measuring or marking, she cut a new patch, exactly the right size, out of a scrap piece of denim. Then she put her left hand up inside the pant leg and with her right hand sewed the patch with firm, even stitches. She loves to help me out in this way. But when it came to advice about vans, she and Dad felt like they had nothing to offer. Both of them were in their fifties when they first learned to drive a car, and motor vehicles are still a mystery to them. So they watched, listened, and kept their opinions to themselves. If we had been shopping for a horse, they would have had volumes of excellent advice.

Knowing his love of history, I took Dad to the Harrisburg Museum one afternoon. Headed by Al and Iris Strutz, the museum is a testimony to their dedication and to the work of many volunteers. Al served as our tour guide. Dad and I stepped into the restored kitchen at the museum, and suddenly our roles reversed. I was tentative and unsure of myself, wondering, "What *is* this stuff?"

Dad acted like he had just come home. "My mother had one like this," he told me, touching the iron fondly. "And like this—it's a slaw-maker, you know, a cabbage cutter."

Ordinary Days

I recognized the cream separator for what it was, but Dad and Al went on to discuss the relative merits of the DeLaval separators versus the McCormick-Deering.

Upstairs in the museum bedroom, we found a little book with all the dates of the year printed inside, and people's names written in old-fashioned script. "A birthday book," Dad explained. "My sisters used to have these to keep track of their friends' birthdays." He flipped a few pages, then stopped. "Noah Mast from Thomas, Oklahoma, 1889. I knew the man."

I couldn't believe it. History at the Harrisburg Museum had reached out and touched my father.

We went on to the farm-equipment building. Dad pointed out one item after another and told me what it was, what it was for, or how much it held. Dad, the wheat farmer from Oklahoma, and Al, the wheat farmer from North Dakota, soon discovered how much they had in common. They walked around the enormous steam engine, affectionately patting it, and reminisced about wheat harvest in the old days. They inspected the threshing machine and Dad guessed, "This probably had a 28-inch cylinder and a 46-inch separator." Sure enough, there, stencilled in faint letters on the side, were the words, "28-inch cyl.—46-inch sep." I kept thinking, *I never knew my dad knew all this stuff.*

It was time to go, but Al wanted to start the motor on a huge, lime-green, cast-iron contraption.

"This was the original irrigation pump out at OSU in the 1890s," Al said proudly. "It still works." He poured in a bit of fuel and positioned a rod. Then he stepped on one spoke of a wheel that was almost as big as he was, grabbed onto another spoke, and slowly turned. We heard a wheezing sound from the motor, then a small pop, then nothing.

"It's okay," I said. "You don't need to start it for us."

But Al, determined, kept turning. "It always starts on the second try," he insisted, puffing slightly. But by the fourth turn nothing had happened.

What should I do? Mom was home with the children and I was sure they were getting hungry. Al gave the wheel another turn. There was another puff, then nothing. Suddenly, this motor seemed symbolic of my parents and their generation—a relic of another era, something wonderful in its heyday but irrelevant, almost pitiful, now.

"We really need to go," I told Dad, and, to Al's disappointment, we edged out the door and climbed into the van.

Dad had barely closed his door when we heard a tremendous BOOM! behind us. Another followed a few seconds later, then more in rapid succession. I looked around, frightened, and saw Al running out of the building, grinning triumphantly, waving his arms.

"It's going!" he yelled. We returned to the green monster, now chuffing and turning in perfect coordination. The wheel turned, the piston pushed, the gears meshed at the right moment. Perfect.

Dad and Al couldn't stop smiling, watching this dead machine come back to life. Did they sense, as I did, that there was something of themselves in this lime-green pump? "Don't give up on us. Give us the right spark, ask us the right questions, listen to us—you'll be amazed at what we have to offer."

Then we came home and there was Mom, bringing to my children's childhood a piece of her own: a paper chain of dancing little girls, holding hands, all their braids connected to each other.

Orval

*I*was almost finished gathering the walnuts from under the tree when a sudden gust of wind sent dozens more thumping to the ground all around me. I was struck, not by a walnut, but by the sudden realization that Orval would never shell my walnuts again.

He used to lower himself stiffly down into a kitchen chair and demand, in the heightened decibels he used for all conversation, "You got any nuds to crag?" I'd bring him a small bucketful and he'd start in, first demonstrating his special pocket-knife technique that split the shell neatly in two without damaging the kernel inside. He'd stop for a bit of lunch, then work steadily until mid-afternoon, when I would insist on his nap.

"You got any more nuds to crag?"

"Why don't you go take a nap?"

"It ain't nap-time! I'm here to shell walnuts! Didn't you know what I'm here for?"

"You're supposed to lie down and put your feet up, aren't you?"

"My feet are right on the ground where they belong. Me sittin' here, this is worthless!"

"What am I going to do if you come next time and I don't have any nuts left?"

"I'll have to sit home, I guess!"

Often I gave up at this point and brought him some more walnuts.

"Oh, thank you, thank you!" Then, in German, cracking contentedly: "One is barefooted and one has no shoes. Now which would you rather be?"

"Barefooted," I'd answer for the twentieth time.

"How come?"

"Because he might have shoes at home."

"Hrah! Hrah! Hrah! Well! Little and smart is worth something, too!"

That was his favorite German expression. I never did figure out what he meant by it.

Orval Smucker was my husband's grandfather, and he died at the age of 94. Paul's sister took care of Orval for four years, and every so often Paul and I would take him for the day to give her a break. Sometimes I'd take him out for coffee at the Hungry Farmer, out by the Harrisburg exit.

There was no sneaking into a booth with Orval. He would shuffle determinedly to the counter, sit on a stool, and holler in his raspy voice for a cup of coffee. Then he'd talk to me.

"This is a Japanese family that owns this, you know," he shouted at me one day between slurps of coffee.

"They all work together. That girl over there is one of theirs. Hey, Sis! You work here, huh? With your family? No, no more coffee. I take it a cup at a time. You know those fellows that bombed that building in Oklahoma City? They're probably gonna electrocute them."

Orval died on a Saturday, and on Tuesday evening, after the viewing, we all went out to Abby's Pizza to celebrate Uncle Milford's birthday. I thought, *Pizza? With Grandpa lying in the funeral home just a few blocks away?* But I went along, not wanting to miss the party. I watched the noisy mixture of Smucker personalities (Family motto: "What's the use of an opinion if you don't state it emphatically?"), and I sensed that Orval would have approved. It was only natural that his descendants would meet at a restaurant to celebrate a birthday, discuss the world, and have a good time. Pizza after a viewing? "Why sure!"

When he got too tottery to go to restaurants, I'd set him at the kitchen table and offer him a cup of coffee.

"Why sure! I alwiz tell'em a cup at a time."

"Do you want sugar?" I'd ask.

"Naw, I quit sugar a long time ago. I had diabeades so I had to quit sugar."

"Do you still have diabetes?"

"Naw, not that I know of. I went to George Kanagy and he cured me of it."

"How did he do that?"

"He gave me food capsules. He tested me. He said, 'You got diabeades, the worst kind.' Well, George said my pancreas gland had quit working. He said, 'You should get a food capsule to strengthen your pancreas gland so it don't pull this trick again.' He got me these food capsules and as far as I know I never had diabeades again. Now you tell me what a food capsule is! I've asked every doctor I've seen and I'm gonna keep asking people—see if I can find somebody that knows. I've never been able to get anyone to tell me, and George is dead and gone."

Today, two of Orval's granddaughters are in medical school. I like to think that a touch of their grandpa's curiosity and persistence inspires them. Maybe someday they will finally discover what was in those mysterious food capsules. Perhaps they will even make sure we can buy Orval's favorite ointment at the pharmacy—something he called DMSO Oil.

Grandpa would follow me around the house, overalls loose on his bony frame, shouting about this wonderful potion.

"Now you cain't buy it in the drugstore, you know. I alwiz get mine from the vet. And every time I get a cut on my hand, I just rub that stuff on and it heals right up. Why sure! And that oil isn't just for the outside of you! That stuff goes through your skin right into your bloodstream. I have no intention of dying of canzer like my neighbor lady did. They say those canzer cells get in your blood. Well! If any would try it on me, that DMSO Oil would kill them right off. Why, one time I found a lump and I was afraid it was canzer so I rubbed DMSO Oil on it and, wouldn't you know, it went away!"

Will Paul be like this in 50 years? I used to worry. Already, I could see similarities sifting through the generations: the bristly eyebrows, the strong nose, the lanky frame. What if Paul ended up this raw, this unrefined, with a whiskery, wobbling chin? On the other hand, what if he ended up this colorful, this full of personality, this undefeated by old age?

It was Orval's sheer orneriness that won me over, almost in spite of himself. That, and the odd honor of my being the only one in the clan who was fluent in his native German dialect of Pennsylvania Dutch. He never did remember my name, but always referred to me as That One That Talks Dutch. Orval would confront me anywhere, especially at quiet places like church, with a wild, *"Vell! Vee geht's?"* (Well! How's it going?) followed by his famous laugh—Hrah! Hrah! Hrah!

As Orval lay dying in a nursing home in Eugene, he turned his head and followed me with his eyes as I entered the room. The nurse was astonished, as he had been unresponsive all morning. Perhaps, she said, it was because he knew I was That One That Talks Dutch. I leaned over his bed and told him good-bye, telling him, in German, to go when it's time to go, not to hang on. But Orval, being Orval, hung on for hours and days longer than anyone thought possible.

At the burial, the grandsons took shovels and, in our faith tradition, helped to fill the grave. I saw in them all, bent to their solemn task, a touch of their hardworking farmer grandpa, always determined to get the job done.

And now, at last, he had finished.

But every October, when walnuts shower from the tree in a gust of wind, I remember him. Little and smart may be worth something, as Orval always said, but old and full of life is worth much more.

Aunts

When my son Matt answered the phone on his 18th birthday a few weeks ago, we heard a staticky but beautiful "Happy birthday to yooooou" warbling from the receiver. The other kids glanced at each other.

"It's Aunt Barb," they said, knowingly.

For years, my husband's sister Barb has called her nieces and nephews on their birthdays. Despite her siblings' growing number of offspring (27 and counting), plus her years of work, college, medical school, and now her residency, Barb has faithfully kept up this tradition.

"Well, see, I'm kind of stuck in my math class," Matt confided, halfway through their conversation. "Did you ever study limits in calculus? It has to do with, like, derivatives."

Barb couldn't help him, but it turned out that she had had the same math teacher at "LB" (Linn-Benton Community College) and, discussing college and calculus, she helped Matt feel like the adult he now officially is.

Barb's conversation with Jenny, whose fifth birthday was two days before, was vastly different from the calculus discussion.

Jenny yelled into the phone, "We had *tea* for my party and we dressed up like *fancy ladies!*" Barb, being the flexible aunt that she is, seemed just as interested in tea and cupcakes as she was in limits and derivatives.

We honor our mothers in May and dads in June, but I think the aunts in our lives deserve recognition as well. Theirs is a pleasant role that, unlike parenting, is as simple or complicated as they choose to make it. Their influence can vary from the simple stability of being there to the profound impact of active involvement.

Aunts experience the love and pride of parenting without the pain or responsibility. I discovered this when I first became an aunt at age 17, when my mother woke me up in the middle of the night and told me my brother and his wife had just had a baby, a girl named Annette.

I am astonished, now, at how many square, Instamatic pictures we took of Annette as a small child—holding a kitten, opening gifts, on our laps. Everything she did was cute and amazing and wonderful. But when she had a messy diaper or was hungry or upset, I plopped her back in her mother's lap.

Today, when I see the funny yet level-headed person Annette has become, I know it's because of her parents' choices, and her own. But, as her aunt, I feel entitled to share in her parents' pride.

With small gestures, aunts make a big imprint on a child's memory. This is why my sister bought a bag of orange marshmallow circus peanuts one summer when she came to visit, and we sat down after supper and ate them slowly and ceremonially.

"Ewww, what's so special about those weird candies?" my daughter wanted to know.

"Aunt Edna used to babysit us when Mom went grocery shopping," we explained, "and she always had this jar of circus peanuts up on the shelf. We thought it was the most wonderful treat in the world."

My daughter didn't understand, of course. But, reverently chewing, we relived that feeling of being indulged and cared for at Aunt Edna's.

Often, in adolescence, we feel trapped in our family's patterns and wonder if we will ever be able to escape. Aunts give us a glimpse of a different way of life, a vivid object lesson that while our genes determine that we might be skinny like the Yoders or stout like the Millers, our choices make the biggest difference, and we are not destined by fate to follow in our parents' footsteps.

Aunt Vina seemed vast and expansive in all the areas where my mother was tight and restrained. She breezed in from Iowa a couple of times a year and greeted us with enveloping hugs; in our family, we didn't hug.

She freely spent money at the grocery store and introduced us to such modern wonders as Hidden Valley Ranch dressing. Who knew something so delicious existed, so unlike Mom's Miracle Whip and vinegar mixtures?

Vina's house was Interior Decorated, a sophisticated term that meant thick carpets, complementary colors, and something very different from the cozy farm-sale-furniture hodgepodge at our house.

That she shared my mother's genes was obvious from looking at her, but Vina showed me that I could be as different from my mother as I chose to be.

The aunts who make the biggest difference are the truly dedicated ones such as Barb and her sister Rosie. They arrange annual activities for all the nieces and nephews—camp-outs, trips to the beach, and jaunts to the hills to play in the snow. Each trip to the coast means elaborate sand castles on the beach, and every ride home brings a long, made-up-as-we-go story from Rosie that my kids remember in vivid detail, even years later.

Most importantly, Barb and Rosie care for the kids on a personal level, aware and concerned. While I appreciate this, I felt a confusing mixture of gratitude and resentment the time Rosie got into a long discussion with the teenage girls during a walk on the beach. They weren't sure they liked being Mennonite, the girls told her, among other dismaying facts that they had never divulged to their mothers. While I was glad my daughter had shared her feelings, I was troubled that she hadn't shared them with me.

When we were in Kenya, the orphan boys we were teaching had been capably cared for by an all-male staff for some time. The atmosphere changed when a young woman named Nancy was hired to be an all-purpose secretary, nurse, and organizer. Suddenly, the boys seemed drawn to her desk, confiding in her, telling her things they had never told the houseparents or anyone else.

We mentioned this to our Kenyan friend Vincent. "She's being their auntie," he said, as though it was perfectly logical. "Traditionally, Mom is the cook and nurse and disciplinarian in an African family, but not the friend and companion. This role is reserved for the auntie."

I don't know how the parents choose the particular auntie, but she takes a personal interest in the child and guides him or her through childhood and adolescence.

I know plenty of mothers who, as I did, suffered from guilt and a sense of inadequacy when their kids confided in another woman. I also have been in the opposite role, when teenage girls told me things they couldn't bring themselves to tell their mothers, and I listened with a sense of guilty betrayal.

Perhaps the Africans are on to something wise, frankly recognizing that Mom cannot always be all things to all people, and that sometimes it's hard to confide in her, and then wisely assigning a specific role to a parent's sibling to meet this need in a child's life.

It didn't take me long to recover when my daughter confided in Rosie, since Rosie was wise and level-headed and would tell me if there was anything I really needed to know. And I had to admit I find it hard to listen to my daughter without lecturing.

Looking back, I now realize that Rosie was truly being an auntie in the African sense.

Mom and Dad deserve the honor they receive in May and June, but I propose we send applause and flowers to the aunts in our lives as well—the ones who give us circus peanuts, the ones who teach us to hug and, most of all, the aunties who listen and care and who remember, 27 times a year, to pick up the phone and sing "Happy Birthday."

Becky

I love this. My sister Becky is 39 years old and I'm only 37.

For most of the year she is only a year older than me, but from June 8 to June 29 she appears to be two years older. She used to remind me of this, in her maddeningly superior way, by spending those three weeks chanting in Pennsylvania German, *"Ich bin 9 un du bisht usht 7!"* (I am 9 and you are only 7.) Or whatever the numbers happened to be.

Of course, Becky was maddeningly superior in many ways. Cool and controlled where I was feisty. Socially adept when I was awkward. And she was pretty. When we were in elementary school, our next-oldest brother Fred would tell Becky that all his friends liked her.

Becky, in turn, would haul me in front of the mirror. "I want to show you how I'm pretty and you're not. See, my face is longer and yours is more round, and Freddy says I'm prettier. And my nose is more straight (Freddy says) and yours points up at the end."

I believed everything she said.

To the rest of the family, we were *de maet*, "the girls," born between three older brothers and another sister six years younger than me.

When we were teenagers, it was Becky's job to reform me. She was constantly adjusting my clothes, telling me to stand up straight, and scolding me for talking too much when her friends were over. We looked a lot alike, enough so that people took us for twins. But mostly I was aware of our differences. She had Dad's thin frame. I had Mom's thick ankles. At school, she spent the lunch hour standing by the heater in the hall, talking with friends. I stayed in the library and read.

Recently I read a T-shirt slogan, "God made us sisters; Prozac made us friends." In our case, it was a wealth of shared experiences that eventually dispelled the rivalry and forged a powerful bond between us.

Like the night of the dripping water tower when we were about 16 and 17. Dad had gone by bus to visit his mother. For some reason Becky and I were chosen to go pick him up in St. Cloud, 40 miles away, at 2 a.m. And, Dad told us on the phone, the bus station was closed so a friendly policeman had taken him to the police station.

We set out, almost alone on the country roads, carefully following the directions Dad gave us. Into town, then a right turn onto a deserted street. This didn't look quite right, but eventually we found a little brick police station, and beside it was the water tower that was supposed to be there, but everything was dark.

We parked the car and cautiously got out. The night was warm and quiet, with a light breeze. We crept to the door and knocked, but no one answered. The water tower loomed high above us, a ghostly silver in the moonlight. Stray drips of water dropped down from high above and swept toward us in the breeze. It was utterly creepy.

We drove the deserted streets, mystified, coming back several times to knock on the door and shiver under the shadow of the hulking water tower. Finally, a young policeman showed up and told us that this was actually Waite Park, a small town at the edge of St. Cloud. He directed us to the right police station, and we found Dad and drove home. But for years we shivered at the memory of the dripping water tower in the night.

Ordinary Days

We went to high school together and were the first in the family to graduate. We worked on the farm together, stacking hay bales, picking rocks, and weeding the garden. We found more and more odd similarities between us, like the fact that we prayed the same fervent silent prayers whenever we worked on the farm: that we would be kept from seeing any garter snakes.

Becky worked at a nursing home during my last year of high school. It was our first experience of being separated, and it was worse when she worked the afternoon shift. When our schedules coordinated again, we'd sit at the kitchen table and talk well into the night. Dad would shuffle by in his pajamas and exclaim, "*Ach, maet,* go to bed!" But he would grin a little bit—glad, I imagine, to see us enjoying each other's company.

Becky left for college the next year. On weekends she'd catch a ride partway home with friends, and I'd go pick her up and bring her home. One afternoon we drove home in a blizzard, with gusts of windblown snow obliterating our view. It took us an hour-and-a-half to drive 25 miles. Another day we were making a left turn and were hit by a car that had suddenly decided to pass us. Becky and I had glanced at each other just as the car hit. Our heads knocked together and we got matching bumps on our foreheads.

I went to live in Oregon while Becky was still in college. I missed her terribly. One year she decided to spend her spring break in Oregon and we arranged to go to the coast for four days. Such a wonderful opportunity—we wanted to make the most of it. First of all, we decided, we wouldn't eat junk food, and we stocked up on veggies and peanut butter. But our motel in Florence happened to be next door to a Dairy Queen. Such an opportunity—we couldn't pass it up. So we limited ourselves to one DQ treat a day.

We grew up without television, so watching TV in a motel was always a big temptation. This time we decided we shouldn't watch—such a waste of time. But, being young and reckless, we checked the *TV Guide,* just in case, and discovered that *Gone With The Wind* was going to be on the exact three nights we were there. Such an opportunity—we couldn't pass that up either. So each evening we sat on the bed with a pile of celery sticks and a jar of peanut butter between us, and watched *Gone With The Wind* for an hour.

Whenever the movie was scary, we ate faster. When Scarlett and Melanie hid under the bridge, we frantically stabbed celery sticks into the peanut butter and crunched faster and faster. When the crazy Yankee soldier came to the house, we were almost too terrified to eat. I hopped off the bed and tested the doorknob to make sure it was locked. The next morning, we discovered that we had left the keys in the other side of the door all night.

Our twenties brought changes for both of us—jobs, marriage, children, moves. In many ways our lives diverged, but the bond between us was strong enough to survive these changes. Our thirties brought more changes, as Becky, her engineer husband, and their son moved to the Middle East. Communication was frustrating—letters were slow and phone calls were expensive. Then came e-mail. Suddenly there was once again an immediacy to our communication, a sharing of casual trivia, like talking over the supper dishes.

As we get older, we keep finding more similarities between us. We both have asthma, we like navy-blue and pink sweaters, and we love to read. In other areas, our roles slowly change. She now envies my nose, as it's smaller than hers. I find myself giving her advice when we go shopping.

Ordinary Days

I have a "Stone Soup" comic strip that I plan to send to Becky next year when she turns 40. Joan tells her sister Val, "You always lorded it over me. You dated first, drove first, left home first. . . ," then she grins and adds, "but now. . . you're going to hit 40 first."

I'll let myself gloat for a while. But, really, it wouldn't be fair to let Becky experience her forties all alone. So, a year and three weeks later, I'll join her.

Oregon Fruit

My children and I and various in-laws are at Oxbow Orchards, picking blueberries. My second bucket is half full and I still gasp at the size of these berries—they hang there like clusters of grapes and slide almost effortlessly into my bucket. My 10-year-old son is down the row, steadily picking. The younger three are gradually picking less and eating more. I can't see them; the bushes are taller than I am. But I hear them calling up and down the rows.

I marvel at my bush and its infinite supply and think of my blueberry-picking attempts six years ago when we lived in Canada. Scruffy little bushes and pea-sized berries, a howling baby in the stroller, and always a wary eye for black bears. Matthew, age 4, who liked to pick but not eat, would hand all his berries to Amy, age 2, who liked to eat but not pick. If I went home with a quart of berries, I was happy indeed.

It's no wonder Grandma used to talk about Oregon like it was the Garden of Eden, I think, popping an enormous berry into my mouth. Grandma and her family had lived in Oregon when she was a teenager. Then they moved back to the Midwest and none of her children or grandchildren had ever come back here to live until I married an Oregonian and eventually we ended up in Oregon. Now I was an awed participant in my in-laws' summer ritual of harvesting and preserving an astonishing parade of fruit.

As I pick, I remember sitting around the kitchen table in Minnesota, making applesauce with the few precious apples available to us. Grandma was across the table spinning tales about a wonderful land out West that was the most beautiful place she had ever seen. Oh, the mountains! (Mountains? I imagined a series of up-ended cones, all snow-capped.) And the fruit. There was no way to describe the wonderful fruit in Oregon. Berries, peaches, pears—almost every kind of fruit you could want. There was so much of it, she couldn't begin to tell us. And it was all lovely, not like these little crabapples we were cutting up.

I jerk to the present and ease out of my bush to check on the children. Matthew has picked almost a gallon, amazing child. Amy has picked half a gallon and gone off to play with her cousin Jessica. The two youngest have given up all pretense of picking and are wandering down the rows, happily eating.

Grandma was the third oldest of 15 children and felt much of the responsibility of providing for them all. She loved to tell of the summer she and her sister Katie picked cherries off their tree and sold them door-to-door in Portland to help support the family. But the cherries wouldn't sell, since all the housewives wanted to know what kind they were and Grandma and Katie didn't know. Finally the sisters had a little conference beside the road and decided to call them Black Pippins. After that they sold them all.

Then Grandma would always tell the story of when they still lived in Minnesota and the only food they had put up for winter was a quart jar of rhubarb. A quart of rhubarb and all those children—I couldn't imagine. How did they survive? Grandma couldn't remember, but somehow God had provided and there she was, still with us. It was no wonder Oregon had seemed like the land of plenty.

I've picked far more blueberries than I ever intended to. We gather the buckets and discarded sweatshirts and reluctantly leave the patch. *Is it possible to appreciate enough the lush bounty of all these berries,* I wonder, *all this food, these well-fed children climbing into the van?*

I pay for the berries and drive away, thinking about my life and Grandma's. My life is so much easier than hers ever was, and it's a lot easier now than when my children were smaller. I worry that I could get so used to all these blessings that I'd start to take them for granted.

Later, running the berries through my hands and into the sink, I somehow feel sure I never will. I see a different kind of fruit, values that Grandma unknowingly handed to me and that I can pass to my children and beyond. I see the value of family, resourcefulness, hard work, and—most of all—a joyful appreciation of all God's gifts.

Traditions

On the first Thanksgiving after Paul and I were married, we gathered at Paul's grandparents' house and everyone slipped into familiar roles.

Paul's mom and the aunts bustled around the kitchen preparing a huge dinner. The young moms chased after toddlers, the teenagers played basketball, and the uncles sat around the living room and talked about farming. I felt nervous and a bit overwhelmed, unsure of my place in this noisy bunch of people.

Sixteen years later, I take my role in the family with the same ease that everyone else did on that long-ago Thanksgiving. I treasure the patterns and rhythms of family, the mix of personalities, the familiarity.

My husband and his six brothers and sisters all happened to be in Oregon at the same time last August, so we gathered at the coast. Anne, my mother-in-law, left the organizing to her daughter, Lois, who hoped to find a house at the coast but felt fortunate, on such short notice, to find a few motel rooms near the beach. All 37 of us came, from Wilton and Anne—now Grandpa and Grandma of the clan—down to the three babies, all born last year.

At the motel, we filled the small living room and overflowed onto the deck. Again, we slipped comfortably into the familiar rituals of family. We moms cooked, walked on the beach, chased toddlers, and put children down for naps. The dads hauled in tents and suitcases, made emergency runs to Safeway, and organized a crabbing trip.

Barb and Rosie, Paul's two single sisters, took all the middle-sized nieces and nephews down to the beach to build elaborate sand castles, a yearly tradition. Enthusiastic kids dug in the sand or scampered for buckets of water. The castles were finished in late afternoon, just as the tide was coming in and, as always, the children hated the thought of all their efforts getting washed away.

"Let's pray!" suggested 10-year-old Emily, so all the children gathered around their castle and prayed that, just this once, God wouldn't let the waves wash it away.

In the evening, we crowded into the living room, ate homemade snacks, and talked. Waves of boisterous little boys rushed through the room as Anne cuddled her grandbabies; Rosie updated us on her frustrating love life; and Wilton and his sons talked about grass seed.

Like waves rolling up on the beach, the familiar rhythms of family surrounded me. But underneath I sensed a troubling current of change. I had thought of it first when Anne relinquished her spot as the family organizer and, instead, Lois coordinated the motel and meals. But I saw other indications as well.

One evening, we cooked up a huge pot of clam chowder. Before every family dinner there is a moment when, almost by instinct, the conversations hush, the children stop playing and join their parents, and Wilton, or whoever is hosting the meal, asks the blessing on the food or chooses someone else to do it. This time, however, we were at a motel, and no one was host. There was a pause—who was in charge? Then Paul said quietly, "Dad, would you ask the blessing?"

It was a simple question, but to me it symbolized another change—Wilton, like his wife, was stepping back and letting someone else take over.

Ordinary Days

We bowed our heads as Wilton led in prayer, but my thoughts were interrupted by my 7-year-old son, who turned to me and whispered, "Mom! Did you ever notice that Grandpa always starts his prayers, 'We thank thee, Lord'?"

I smiled and nodded. Like the sand castle that washed away despite the children's prayers, changes had come to this family in the last 16 years. But like the sand and the sea, their faith and love—and Grandpa's prayers—hadn't changed a bit.

Places

Angels on Interstate 5

grew up on a farm beside a gravel road in Minnesota, where I learned to wave at every passing car when I was working outside, and at every vehicle I met when I was driving. Not to wave was to be stuck-up, unfriendly, unneighborly.

Now, in Oregon, a narrow cow pasture separates our home from I-5. We are close enough to hear every car that goes by and read brand names on motorhomes, but too far away to distinguish faces. We are close enough to wave, but we don't.

When we first moved to this house, the constant stream of traffic made me vaguely apprehensive. It never stopped. The roar of passing vehicles was always there, and when I went to bed at night I could still see a long line of headlights coming from the south. I wanted to go out on the overpass and hang up a sign: GO HOME AND GO TO BED.

For the first weeks I didn't like to be home alone with the children after dark. I felt vulnerable, this close to all those passing people. One of them might be waiting for a chance to harm us. My logical husband finally convinced me that this was unlikely. If someone wanted to hurt us, they would not bother to climb a fence, find their way through a pasture, and stumble over an electric fence in the dark to do so.

So my fears and apprehensions eased and the freeway traffic became part of the scenery. Now I seldom notice vehicles, and the noise fades into the background. Although thousands of people drive by every day, they seem like faceless forms, insulated from my life even though they pass nearby. I suppose we are only part of the scenery to them, a farmhouse between Eugene and Albany.

But, to my delight, every now and then someone emerges from the background to become a real person whose life connects with ours.

Our children's pastime of "honking trucks" was our first way of communicating with individual drivers. Of course, the children think of it only as a fun diversion on walks. We stop on the overpass above the northbound lanes, and they pump their fists in the air and wait anxiously to see how many trucks honk their horns. Many of them oblige. From the smiles on their faces, I can tell the moment makes my children and the truck drivers equally happy.

Apparently some of these truck drivers have decided to keep honking at us, because every day I hear a honk or two from passing trucks. It makes me feel like I'm back in Minnesota, with friendly neighbors waving as they drive by. Mentally I wave back—Hello to you, too, whoever you are.

Sometimes a freeway misfortune brings drivers to our door—a car breakdown, running out of gas. We hand them the phone or a container of lawn mower gasoline. Without exception they are grateful and generous, insisting on paying $5 for a gallon of gas. Are these people the angry drivers that crowd my back bumper on I-5? If they are, they turn into likable people when they are out of their vehicles and we meet on our front porch.

We try to be as helpful as possible, not only to be neighborly, but also because the Bible reminds us that the strangers we help may be angels in disguise. So after some-one leaves, our family starts guessing—were they or weren't they? The young couple who landed in the ditch. . .hmmm . . .do angels have blue hair and rings in their noses? Who knows? Or maybe it was the well-dressed businessman who ran out of gas. Or the desperate fellow who was late for a job interview.

One evening my husband worked late and the children and I were eating outside at the picnic table. Two young men walked in from the freeway. They had been pulling a car on a trailer and it slid off, so could they have some boards to make a ramp to load the car again? I found a few of my husband's 2x6s for them, then offered them some of the tacos I had made for supper.

"No thanks," they said, "but we'd take some ice water." I gave it to them, and as they turned to leave they offered to pay for the boards. This time I said "no thanks" but said my husband would appreciate if they returned the boards or placed them where we could easily get them.

As soon as they left, the speculating began. Weren't they nice? Mom, do angels eat? Surely it was a sign of angel-ness to forgo the tacos but drink the water. Now, the crucial test—would they return the boards or not? (Why would they need 2x6s in heaven?) The children waited anxiously, but the young men never returned and the boards disappeared. Too bad. Maybe next time.

As I said, most of the time I-5 fades into the background of our lives. But we never know when someone will emerge from the freeway to become a real person with a face and personality. So we listen for the honk, we answer the knock on the door, and we watch for angels.

1000-Story House

My husband and I sat in an office in Albany and signed a bewildering array of papers for 45 minutes. When we finished, the house was ours.

I remember when I'd first drive by this house, nearly 20 years ago. It always came looming at me on one of the sharp curves on Powerline Road, near Harrisburg—a plain, boxy, white farmhouse, with only a few small trees beside it to soften the sharp edges. It looked like a child's block, tossed onto the corner of a kitchen table.

What I didn't realize was that the house belonged to Wilton and Anne Smucker, whose son I'd marry three years later.

Paul and I have lived in nine houses in the last 15 years, from an apartment in Woodburn, Oregon, to a cabin in the Canadian bush, to a farmhouse whose dining room was once a chicken house. We enjoy travel, new experiences, other cultures.

In the last few years, however, we find ourselves wanting to home in, settle down, and find a place we can make our own. Too soon, our children will be off on adventures of their own. We want them to leave with a sense of place, of roots, of their role in the family history.

So we are buying Paul's parents' house, that plain, square house on Powerline Road. It is, I have discovered, a two-story house with a thousand stories.

According to my father-in-law, the house was built in 1911 by a man named Daniel Kropf. It has been in the family ever since. Now, Daniel's great-great-grandchildren will be moving into it.

I hope someday one of my kids will find the bullet hole. Back in the height of World War I, the story goes, Daniel was bishop of the Harrisburg Mennonite Church down the road. Not only did he preach in German, but he discouraged his flock from joining the Army. His views didn't make him popular in the community, of course, and one morning Daniel found a yellow stripe painted around the church and the doors padlocked shut. Not long after that, someone came by and shot at Daniel's house. The hole is still there, somewhere, the family says.

Daniel's granddaughter Elsie was next to live in the house, with her husband Vernon and their six little Knox sons, who turned out to be the Knox Brothers, well-known Southern-Gospel singers.

I'm sure my children will wonder about the funny-looking fiberboard rectangles all over the walls and ceilings of two of the bedrooms upstairs. I'll tell them that Elsie's son Wayne and his family were the next ones to live there, and those rooms were the Knox Brothers' sound studio. If my kids think the fiberboard looks funny, I suppose they should have seen the walls when they were also covered with egg cartons to further improve the acoustics.

The house was transferred to a different branch of the family tree in 1979. Daniel Kropf, the original builder, had a son, Frank, who married a widow named Annie Smucker. Annie had two young sons named Orval and Herman from her first marriage. Orval turned out to be my husband's grandfather, but first he and Herman gave the family tree a violent twist when they married their step-father Frank's younger sisters.

Ordinary Days

I've had this explained to me a dozen times by the great-aunts, but I still have to draw diagrams on the back of an envelope when my 6-year-old asks me how he is related to his little friend Spencer. (Let's see, Spencer would be a grandson of Frank and Annie's son Lloyd, so *this* way you would be third cousins, and *that* way you're half second cousins once removed.)

So in 1979, Orval's son Wilton and his wife Anne bought the house, relocated it a mile up the road, and moved in with their seven children. They turned the house 180 degrees in the process, forever confusing the relatives who stopped in, who would gesture toward the bay window that they needed to run in to Harrisburg, when actually Harrisburg was toward the kitchen. Wilton's family also removed the egg cartons (filling a tin can with tacks, recalls Anne) and turned the sound studio into two bedrooms.

I entered the picture at this point, some months after I saw the house for the first time, when I got to know Wilton and Anne's daughter Barb. We'd sit crosslegged on the beds in the bedroom at the top of the stairs and talk for hours with the sun shining through the leaves of the walnut tree and into the tall windows. Barb did her best that summer to match me up with her handsome brother Paul, who had just finished his first year of teaching and was working nights in Wilton's grass-seed warehouse. Unfortunately, I seldom saw him because he spent his days sleeping in the southeast bedroom with the shades drawn tight.

My children love the story of the first time I ate a meal at "Grandma's house." We were sitting around the oval kitchen table one evening, just as we would so many times in the future. The china cabinet was behind me and the two potted philodendrons twined up to the ceiling and then on around the room. Anne was hopping out of her chair every minute or two to make sure everyone was properly served. Paul was there that night, and after the meal he impressed me enormously when he politely thanked his mother for the dinner. (So you see, children, it always pays to mind your manners!)

That was my first meal with the family, I tell the kids, and thankfully the only one where I dropped my ice cream into my lap when dessert was served. I managed to keep cool and Paul never noticed. But eventually Barb's efforts paid off and he noticed me. And now here we are, 18 years later, getting ready to move into that same house. It still looks just like it always has, except now it looks like home.

And the house is ready, too, waiting for our children to come and create a thousand stories of their own.

Road Trip

We pulled into our driveway at 7 on a Friday evening. I sang the "Hallelujah Chorus," and the kids burst from the van in a jubilant explosion. First we wandered through the house and around the yard, getting reacquainted with our home. Then we carried our luggage into the house and put everything away—shoes into closets, dirty sweatshirts into hampers, and the mayo into the fridge.

I also pulled out the memories and looked at them, one by one, then tucked them away where I could easily find them again: bubbles on Bear Tooth Pass, a penny in pickle juice, heads of styrofoam and heads of stone, a waterless day in Wisconsin, and my daughter's "Grandma's House Gazette." Good memories, and also some not-so-pleasant memories, that I hoped, with time, would turn into something positive.

Taking our family on a four-week road trip, after school and before harvest, seemed like a good idea last winter. By the middle of May, however, I wasn't so sure. The preparations seemed endless, and my list grew to five pages: "Ask Kropfs to mow the lawn. Find someone to keep Matt's hamster. Pack: sleeping bags, contact-lens solutions, atlas, flashlight, sandwich supplies, diapers." I weighed all this preparation against what I hoped to accomplish: Seeing people and places, making memories, getting away, reflecting.

My sister-in-law warned me that driving to the Midwest from Oregon is like putting your whole family in the bathroom and staying there for three days.

Actually, all the hours in the van were less stressful than we expected. Except for the times Emily and Ben played Trouble and disagreed every 28 seconds about which way the dice lay, most of us got along. As the hours and miles stretched on, we often settled into a sort of hypnosis, lost in our own thoughts, focusing on tiny details. Like Emily's penny, which I think of now sometimes when I put dill pickles on sandwiches. We found the penny, battered and tarnished, at a rest area in Iowa on our way home. Emily wanted to polish it.

"I need vinegar and salt, right, Mom?"

"Right," I told her, "and we don't have either one, so you'll have to wait until we get home."

But Emily persisted, holding the penny in her hand and thinking of creative alternatives. "Hey, the pickles!" she exclaimed, miles later. "Isn't there vinegar in the dill pickle juice?"

There was. We dropped the penny into a cup and poured the green liquid over it. Now: salt. We pondered for more hypnotic miles, then found an answer: the crumbs at the bottom of the pretzel bag. The penny soaked in this mess, and slowly Lincoln's head became visible.

Lincoln's head was much more obvious at Mt. Rushmore. Of course we had seen their pictures many times, but it was nothing like actually seeing those massive stone faces gazing out of the mountain. Sadly, the visitor's center, with its detailed displays on how this incredible project was completed, was almost deserted. In contrast, the gift shop, with its T-shirts and toothpick holders, was so full of people that I wouldn't let the children leave my side for fear I'd lose them in the crowd.

I admit, our skulls weren't exactly made of inch-thick styrofoam for the first half of our trip, but some of us felt like they were as we endured the pressure changes in the mountains while battling sore throats and earaches. Getting sick on vacation is an experience that, we hope, will eventually redeem itself as having drawn the family closer together, built our characters, or something equally valuable. During our week in Canada, as we visited, canoed, and fished in the area where we used to live, we discovered that the doctor shortage there is now so acute that even the doctors that delivered my babies refused to see us. So we altered our plans and headed for the best hospital in the world—Mom's house.

My parents' place in Minnesota is like the stereotypical "Grandfather's Farm" (red barn, white house, one cow, five chickens) featured in many of the storybooks I used to read to the children. It is also a restful retreat for adults, a place of endless discovery for kids, and a gold mine of memories. The young cousins explored Grandpa's haymow, hunted for kittens, and built a fort with straw bales. Amy discovered an old Royal typewriter in the basement and pounded out copies of a little newspaper she named the "Grandma's House Gazette."

"Sara Yoder (Grandma) made cinnamon rolls today," she wrote. "They smelled and tasted delicious. They are not available for sale, but if you ask for one, Grandma will probably give you one." She also noted, "Today there were several interesting games played in Grandma's basement. The noisiest ones were Rubber Band Fights and Mouse Trap. The rubber band fights were terminated because one player was harmfully injured."

The "harmfully injured" child was typical of the health crises we faced in Minnesota—momentarily frightening but turning out fine in the end. One of Dad's lambs was bottle-feeding so enthusiastically one day that it pulled the nipple off the bottle and swallowed it. A nephew ate a bad hot dog at my brother's house and threw up 40 or 50 times that night. Thankfully the rubber band fighter, the lamb, the nephew, and our family all recovered, and we left for Wisconsin refreshed and rested.

Paul's brother Phil and his family live in the middle of Wisconsin's dairy country. The electricity went off one morning while the last piece of toast was in the toaster. With 10 children, lots of mud and puddles, and no water in the faucets, we found it almost impossible to keep clean. Seven-year-old Ben, hunting for earthworms in the pasture, stepped in a fresh cow pie. Without electricity, he couldn't hose off his feet. I held the reeking shoe at arm's length and reminded myself that making memories was one of my goals for this trip.

I have a feeling that in summers to come, when I drink a glass of lemonade, I will also remember the children's business venture in Wisconsin. Ben and his cousin Caleb wanted to set up a lemonade stand and wouldn't give up, despite the obvious limitation of not having running water in the house.

"Mom, can we have a lemonade stand now?" they persisted. "Huh? Please? Can we mix up some lemonade now? Huh? Can we?"

At one point Caleb flew into the kitchen and grabbed a small bucket and funnel-type filter that they use for milking goats, then dashed off. Later, Ben informed me that they got the bright idea to take water from a puddle in the driveway, put it through the milk filter, and use it for making lemonade. They tasted the water and, hey, it wasn't bad. I was sure they'd get diarrhea or worse. Eventually, we got water from the neighbors, the lemonade was mixed, and the boys earned $1.20. And they didn't get sick.

Ordinary Days

We had taken along jump ropes, Frisbees, and a scooter to occupy the children at rest stops. We also took a spill-proof bottle of bubble soap for 2-year-old Jenny. Over and over, at rest areas all over the West, the older kids tried to teach her to hold the wand to her mouth, "No, Jenny, not *on* your mouth. Right in front, like this. And blow out, not in!" But Jenny couldn't seem to understand.

Years ago, my parents drove over Bear Tooth Pass, near the northeast entrance to Yellowstone Park, and Mom tried to describe it to me.

"You just go up and up and *up!*" she said. "I never saw anything like it. Oh, it's just . . . ." and she shook her head, unable to find the words.

Intrigued, we decided to try that route into Yellowstone. First, we found ourselves in a deep valley, with towering mountains on all sides. Looking around, we realized that the mountain to our left, impossibly steep and high, had a road on it. We caught glimpses of switchbacks—there . . . and up there . . . and oh, look, way up there! Was it actually our route, and would we actually end up way up there on top? Incredible.

We began ascending, grinding slowly up and up, stopping often to look way down below where we'd come from, and gasping at how far we still had to go. Then we'd move on, gradually upward. As we rounded one particularly awesome curve, with all of us gazing, open-mouthed, out the windows, we suddenly became aware of bubbles, a gentle whoosh of soap bubbles that drifted, sparkling, inside the front half of the van. We had been focused on the scenery outside, but now our attention was jerked back inside. Where did these bubbles come from?

Jenny, of course.

She sat in her car seat, grinning triumphantly. In the middle of Bear Tooth Pass, with everyone's attention elsewhere, Jenny had somehow reached the bubble soap and learned, all on her own, to blow bubbles. When we reached the top of the mountain, we felt like we were on top of the world. Jenny, proudly clutching the bubble wand, was without a doubt on the very top of hers.

In all, we traveled almost 7,000 miles and spent nine nights in motels, with all seven of us in one room.

Emily yelled, "Oh, no, I can't find my other sandal!" before approximately 18 rest stops. We saw 13 moose, and we ate at least 50 cheeseburgers.

Was it worth it? I ask myself now, looking over my five-page list one last time before I toss it. *Did I meet my goals?*

Yes, but maybe what really matters is that in the end we still loved each other, all of us were utterly happy to come back home, and we have a new file of memories, safely tucked away where we can easily find them again.

Winds of Change

A cold wind sweeps under the Burnside Bridge as my daughter Amy and I wander from booth to booth at Portland's Saturday Market. It's early—not yet 9—and people are still setting up: wind chimes, pottery, velvet hats. I buy a blue spoon rest to put on the kitchen stove at home—something to remind me of today. Then we walk on, shoulders hunched in the cold.

I remember that a warm wind was blowing the night Amy was born, almost 13 years ago. It was close to midnight when we left for the hospital. As I shuffled to the car, leaning on my husband's arm, the wind blew in over the meadow by our house, soothing and refreshing me.

In the pool of our lives, our first child was a rock that landed in the middle with a huge splash. Amy, two years later, was a leaf that fluttered down and floated gently on top. Those first few years she was tiny for her age, with a cloud of red-gold curls on her head—a quiet, calming presence in our lives.

Amy was never as talkative as her siblings. Instead, she stood back and watched the action, then came to me and carefully summed it up in a concise sentence or two, astonishing me with her vocabulary.

"Matthew turned on the faucet and my dress got all wet," she told me one day when she was barely 2. She wrote me her first note before she was 4 years old—I love U Mom—the word "love" represented by a fat, uncertain heart.

Until she was about 11, I thought Amy would always be this way—quiet, observant, affectionate. Then, like a sudden, chilling gust of wind, she began to change. I first noticed the physical changes, as she grew taller and sturdier. Next came a disquieting stage where she compared me with her friends' moms.

"Phebe's mom makes really good tetrazzini, Mom. Maybe you should get her recipe. Yours is okay but it tastes, well, kind of weird.

"Oh, Mom, can't you do something about those open shelves in the bathroom, with all our towels and stuff?

"When I grow up I want to be like Rita becasue she has lots of little children but she still has a clean house."

That stage soon passed, but the changes continue. She tries on personalities like outfits, switching moods and interests from day to day. I look at her and wonder what happened to the child I knew, how I should respond, who she will become. I seek for ways to reach her, for things we have in common.

This trip to Portland was my husband's idea. A few years ago, he suggested that I take each of our children on an expedition of some sort when they are 12 years old, and then he'll take them on a trip when they're 13. Bonding and memories, you know, and time spent one-on-one.

So, here we are, wandering the Saturday Market because the Lloyd Center doesn't open until 10. We caught the 6:30 Amtrak out of Albany, sipping tea and orange juice from the bistro car as the train swished past Woodburn. The Lloyd Center is our main destination for the day because Amy is "into" shopping. I seldom enjoy shopping, but this is her day; we'll shop.

We are two country girls in the big city, bent on adventure, finding our way together. Our map is our lifeline and we consult it often, our heads bent close together, our fingers touching on the bus routes.

Ordinary Days

We find the MAX stop near the Saturday Market and together we figure out how to get our tickets from the machine. Amy pushes the buttons; I insert a $10 bill. To our delight, the machine blesses us with a shower of Sacajawea coins in change, our first ones. We inspect them together, oblivious to the cold wind and the people around us.

I notice one of Portland's famous rose gardens on the map, not far from where we're going, and wonder if Amy would like to see it. "I mean, the roses wouldn't be blooming yet but I'm sure it would still be pretty."

"Mom, the Rose Garden is where the Blazers play basketball," Amy says quietly, like you would explain something to your grandma. She's right—and there it is, a big arena.

I need a map for this relationship, I think, *with all the routes marked.* When do I give in and when do I stand firm? Should I hug her if she says she doesn't want to be hugged? I want signs to indicate the landmarks: what will matter 20 years from now? What won't? Most of all, I wonder how to connect with this person she is becoming—confident, outgoing, with friends and interests (like Blazers basketball) apart from mine.

At the Lloyd Center, we wander from store to store, looking at clothes. She has Eddie Bauer tastes; I prefer Goodwill. At Sears, we buy her an outfit that's a nice compromise between her tastes, my tastes, and our budget. She hugs the package and thanks me, her eyes shining.

We take the MAX back to downtown and pore over the map at our table at Baskin-Robbins. We have an hour left— where should we go? Amy discovers a Daisy Kingdom logo on the map and wonders if I'd like to go there. Daisy Kingdom is the home of some of the prettiest fabrics in the country—of course I'd like to go. I used to dream of the day when Amy and I would plan projects together and shop for patterns and fabrics. We set out, standing on street corners to get our bearings, the map flapping in the wind.

Before long I am rummaging through stacks of fabrics in the discount room at Daisy Kingdom, lavishly promising Amy that she can have any she wants. Just as I discover a table of angelic pastels, I take a good look at Amy and realize that she is . . . bored.

"It's just that this fabric is kind of babyish," she explains.

She's right, of course. Most of Daisy Kingdom is designed for the preschool crowd. Her comment forces me to face the truth and my own disappointment: she is no longer a little girl, and despite all my hopes, she doesn't share my passion for sewing.

We walk the remaining blocks to the train station, Amy leading the way. The ride home is quiet; both of us are tired. Long after dark, we pull into our driveway, safe at home. She sits on the couch and shows everyone her purchases, telling about our day, flicking her long, red-gold braid over her shoulder.

I watch her, thinking about who she is and who she is becoming. All in all, this has been a beautiful journey, being her mom. She will go places I will never go, but I believe she will always find her way back home, a warm and gentle wind blowing into my life, soothing and refreshing.

Muddy Creek

I'm looking at ordinary things in a new way these days, making a conscious effort to be like my son and not—God bless her anyhow—like my aunt.

In 1983, after I had lived in Oregon for two years, I went back home to Minnesota for a year. One weekend my mother and I drove down to Kalona, Iowa, to spend a few days with relatives—Mom's, mostly, but we also made a dutiful trek to Dad's sister Erma's house.

Erma was Amish, and one of the most talkative people I have ever known. She would lean forward with her chin in one hand and with two fingers pushing into her cheek, talking steadily and batting her eyelashes.

When we arrived, we seated ourselves in her dining room and I took the hickory rocker she offered me. After one attempt at conversation—that was instantly interrupted by Erma—I gave up on talking and decided to keep track of how often she interrupted my mother. In the next hour, Mom made exactly five attempts to speak but never got to finish a sentence. Each time, Erma cut her off mid-sentence and went rattling on.

Somewhere in this amazing monologue, Erma told us about her Western Trip, which is a sort of pilgrimage that many Midwesterners make at least once in their lifetimes. The Amish, who don't have cars or cameras, hire a driver and come home with souvenirs of Yellowstone Park, the coast, and the redwoods. Mennonites come home with slides that they show at family gatherings, and everyone is awed by this incredible geography, so different from the cornfields of Iowa.

Erma batted her eyelashes at me. "Oh, you were in Oregon, weren't you? We were in Oregon on our Western Trip, and we went to see a nice pond."

I thought, *Pond? A pond is where cows come to drink. Why on earth would she have gone to see a pond in Oregon?*

I didn't ask her, of course; I didn't have a chance. Erma must have noticed my puzzled expression because she said, "I have a picture of that place in Oregon," and gestured at a calendar on the wall. And there was a photograph of Crater Lake.

"Be gentle with your judgments of Erma," my dad always said. "She never had the opportunities you've had."

Erma died a few years later. As it turned out, she had the opportunity to see Crater Lake long before I did, and I thought of her recently when we took a quick family vacation and I looked out over Crater Lake for the very first time. Words were inadequate, so I drew in a deep breath of the cold air and exhaled in a long, enchanted "Ahhhhhhh." We drove around the lake and looked at it from a dozen different angles, amazed and awed.

I saw another body of water for the first time not long ago. Not that I hadn't looked at Muddy Creek a thousand times, but that day I really saw it. Our 7-year-old son Benjamin had begged me for weeks to walk along the creek with him so he could show me all his favorite places to play. Finally, one hot afternoon, I took the time to go with him.

Crossing the road, I was in charge, making sure we looked both ways. But as soon as we crossed, he became the guide and I followed.

Gingerly, I followed him through the gap under the fence. He led me across the pasture, hot and dry in the sun, to the welcome coolness of the shade along the creek. Muddy Creek was wide, dark, and slow, with clumps of soft green moss growing at the edges and bits of sunlight sprinkled on top of the water.

Ben found the cow path and bounced along in his black sandals, stopping abruptly to show me his favorite spots. "Here's where I skip rocks. And one time I skipped a rock that was not round and not square! It was a triangle!

"Here are our forts. There's Emily's and here's mine."

Forts? I looked closer. Pieces of wood were stacked up beside one tree, an old coffee can stuck in the roots by another. All the hours he and his sister spent playing at their forts, and this is what they were?

Ben bounced on, running ahead, then coming back to tell me more. I could tell he felt at home here, that he was in love with this world of quiet creek and tall trees and flickering sunlight.

"I want to build a raft and go floating down the creek," he said. "I'll build it like a pallet and put jugs inside to make it float.

"Pretty soon we'll get to the bridge Dad made," Ben announced. And there it was, an old telephone pole laid across the water. I inched across, wanting to look at my feet but getting dizzy from the dark water flowing underneath. Ben reassured, "The water isn't very deep here, so if you fall in, it's okay."

Across the creek, the grass was taller and tangled bushes grew along the water. "Here's where I pick blackberries," Ben told me, "and there's our warehouse—sometimes I stop in to see Dad."

He led me past the warehouse, down to the ford, where the little cousins go swimming. For the next half hour, he showed me how to float with the current and hunt water skippers, long-legged spidery bugs that prance on the surface of the water. Then it was time to go home, with seeds from the dry grass clinging to our wet feet, past the warehouse, along the creek, over the bridge, among the trees, under the fence, across the road, and home.

I thought a lot about Ben and the creek over the next few days. I had never known that he found so many things to do along Muddy Creek, that he loved it so much, that when he looked at it he saw not an ordinary little creek but a magical river of possibilities.

To me, Muddy Creek had always been, well, just Muddy Creek. Maybe I wasn't so different, after all, from Aunt Erma, who looked at Crater Lake and saw a nice pond.

Oregon Coast

I always know when we need a trip to the coast. Whenever the daily details of dishes and bills and overdue library books close in like a cloud of mosquitoes, or when the irritations in our marriage become larger than the things we appreciate, I know it's time.

I found myself at that point in mid-January. Paul, who is practical and efficient, picked up his phone and calendar, and three days later, we were headed west, the tightly coiled wires in my head slowly unwinding as we drove through the hills.

Somehow, I finished the complicated logistics of leaving five children for two days and I could relax at last, leaning my seat back for a nap as Paul drove and the sun broke through the clouds like a heavenly blessing.

I knew I'd feel even better when I got rid of the two pillows in the black garbage bag in the back seat.

My husband stole them last August.

We had spent the night at the LaurenSea Motel south of Newport, a homey place where the owners happily accommodate large families and the children can walk to the beach without crossing the road. We were all packed up to leave when Paul and I made a last sweep through our suite.

While I looked under beds for socks, he snatched the two pillows off the hide-a-bed, thinking they were ours, and stuffed them in the back of the van. I found them that evening when we unpacked. Horrified, I immediately called the motel to explain.

"Yes, my husband noticed they were gone," Mrs. Motel said, a bit coldly, not that I blamed her. "But you don't need to pay for them," she added. "Just return them the next time you come to the coast."

In a special jar in my mind, I accumulate our times at the ocean, much like the jar of seashells in our pantry that collects another precious shell or two every time we return from the beach. I knew the story of Paul and the pillows would eventually be funny, a story I could pull out and chuckle over for years, at Paul's expense.

One of the most vivid memories in my collection is the first time I saw the Pacific Ocean, when I was 19 years old. Coming from the Midwest, I pictured it as a glorified lake.

Nothing could have prepared me for that overwhelming moment of walking across the beach and seeing the ocean: a vast, churning, gray expanse that went on and on until it melted into the horizon.

Enormous waves surged inland, one after another, bulging out of the water and rising up and up until suddenly, the top edge folded over and the whole thing collapsed, roaring to shore with an angry, terrifying power. Then, each wave dissolved into a thin sheet of water on the sand that kept coming and coming, right at me, like it was determined to sweep me into an infinite restlessness. And all around me, I heard a deep, solemn, unending roar that seemed to fill the universe.

It was stunning, overpowering, beautiful.

Everything about the coast had a rugged and frightening beauty—the enormous logs lying placidly on the beach, far out of reach of the waves, but a reminder of the power of the winter storms that tossed them there. Cliffs that reared up harshly at the edge of the beach. Cape Perpetua Lookout, looming hundreds of feet above us, and the Devil's Churn down below, where the force of the waves was constricted into a narrow, rocky channel and the water rolled and boiled with a living fury.

Nothing had the peaceful, manageable beauty of sheep grazing in the Willamette Valley's grass fields, or the well-behaved lakes back in Minnesota, where trees on the opposite shore gave perspective, and small waves lapped delicately at the edges.

The ocean seemed too fierce and uncontrollable for affection, that first day. But since then, I have come to love it, not like I enjoy lilacs and country roads, but more like I love God, with a healthy dose of fear and respect.

Now, we go to the coast for many reasons—for fun, for refreshment, for perspective, or simply for tradition. Each trip is the same and each is different; each is a shell to drop into my jar and cherish, afterward.

I go to a church ladies' retreat every February, in a house overlooking the ocean. There, two dozen women relax and rediscover themselves, laughing hysterically, eating and baring their souls in quiet conversations.

Some summers, we drive to a house on the coast with a vanload of adolescents, children from church who memorized 50 Bible verses to earn three days of camp.

We try to keep up with them, and at 2 a.m., we massage our muscles, sore from hiking, and try to fall asleep while the girls giggle upstairs and the boys in the living room make dreadful noises and muffle their laughter with sleeping bags and pillows.

The coast is one place where it's perfectly acceptable to do something for no other reason than because we've always done it this way.

The annual aunts-and-cousins' day at the beach always, *always*, includes sand castles, a shivering dip in the ocean, taffy at Aunt Belinda's in Newport, ice cream at the Dairy Queen in Philomath, and made-up stories from Aunt Rosie all the way home—for anyone who can stay awake to hear them.

I save a certain jacket for the beach, a hooded gray sweatshirt perfect for walks in the wind and rain. A garage sale find, it reads Santa Clara Women's Basketball on the front, a logo that always amuses the teenage nephews when the whole Smucker clan assembles at the beach.

"How's your team doing?" one of them asks me.

Another one adds, "Did you make a touchdown at your practice last night?"

"Touchdown?" I ask. "Isn't that football?" They laugh, surprised. Aunt Dorcas is sharper than they realized.

We go to the coast for perspective. The petty details are left behind, and, in the vast scope of the ocean, we rediscover what's truly important. The moist wind whips the dust and cobwebs out of my mind and leaves behind only what's strong and solid.

Often, I take along things to do—a book to read, a letter to write, a cross-stitch project. I never get them done. These things belong to my life in the valley, where keeping busy and getting things done seem desperately important. At the coast, they diminish in size and the things that matter—friendships, marriage, God, and family—regain their true significance.

Most of all, I enjoy the times that Paul and I get away by ourselves.

A marriage can get tired over time, frayed with silent anger and bruised with small irritations. Away from the daily patterns of behavior, we talk things out and find ways to change and heal.

Ordinary Days

We went to nearby Florence in January, where we walked on the beach and stayed at Driftwood Shores, keeping the balcony door ajar all night so we could listen to the waves.

The next day, we wandered around Old Town Florence, and Paul waited with unusual patience while I explored the little art galleries.

Then we headed up the coast toward Newport, each curve in the road bringing another scene of damp green mountainsides or waves draping themselves over rocks and sand.

At the LaurenSea Motel, I hauled the black garbage bag to the front door.

"Ah, yes, the pillow thieves," said Mrs. Motel.

I apologized. She smiled. We left.

Normally, I would have felt irritated at Paul for wanting me to return the pillows to the office. After all, he stole them. But this was at the coast, so it didn't seem important. Hadn't he indulged me at the art galleries?

What really mattered was having the pillows off my conscience and going home, refreshed and rested, to drop another seashell in my jar.

Lessons

The Cat
Who Came
to Stay

O n my morning walks, earlier this summer, I often
saw a cat slip into the tall grass beside Substation
Drive. Figuring she belonged to Aunt Susie down
the road, I didn't give the cat much thought except to notice
that she looked like a registered Holstein cow with that pure
white fur with distinct black patches.

Our children had been asking for a cat off and on ever since
we moved into this house. I always said no, knowing that cats
on this corner never lived long because of all the traffic. I did-
n't need the guilt of seeing the children get attached to a cat
and then having it hit by a seed truck. Furthermore, I didn't
want a cat using the sandbox for a litter box.

But one day, out of the blue, the black-and-white cat
decided to invade our lives. I saw her sitting on the front
porch one morning, looking mournfully at the front door.
She meowed piteously when she saw me, "Mwarrr . . .
Please help me. Pleeeeease."

"What do you want, *Katz?*" I asked in Pennsylvania
German, since cats understand it better than English. But
the cat didn't answer.

Where did this animal come from, and why did she pick
us? I checked for a collar. None. I called Aunt Susie. No, it
wasn't hers. The cat looked healthy, and showed no signs of

pregnancy or of kittens. And she couldn't be hungry, as the children fed her bread, milk, and tuna—Bumble Bee, not store-brand. If she was looking for a husband, why did she pick our catless house? She wasn't dumped here, I reasoned, because I had seen her in the neighborhood for weeks.

"Go home, *Katz*," I told her. "We don't need a cat, or want one either. Why are you hanging around here?"

But the cat refused to go, and every day she sat on the porch and meowed at me reproachfully. She reminded me of *Gokum*, the way she marched into my life uninvited and wouldn't leave.

I first saw Bertha—"*Gokum*"—11 years ago when we moved onto a First Nations reservation in Canada to teach school. Her husband was the village chief, and they owned the little cabin we moved into, next door to their house. We called her *Gokum*, Cree for Grandma.

I came to the village with lofty ideals and high expectations, full of wisdom that I was eager to share with the local people. *Gokum's* stern face and piercing black eyes soon let me know that she thought I was the ignorant one, a silly white lady who didn't know how to take care of her own children. Since *Gokum's* English was as limited as my Cree, she used her grandchildren as go-betweens.

We lived on the shore of a lake, and the children were delighted to find that our house was surrounded by sand. On our second day there, the children sat beside the front steps digging in it.

"Our *gokum* says your children shouldn't play in the sand," the grandchildren told me. "They might get sand in their eyes."

"Don't let her intimidate you," my husband Paul said. "Of course they can play in the sand."

So, trembling, I let them. Soon I heard a swishing on the front steps. *Gokum* was sweeping the sand off the steps, muttering angrily.

A few days later a stiff wind blew in. Walking down to the lake for water, Paul noticed a string tied across the path, a foot or so above the ground.

"Our *gokum* did that," the grandchildren explained. "Your children aren't supposed to go farther than that when it's windy and the waves are high."

I was humiliated and furious. Did she actually think I didn't know enough to keep my children away from the lake on a stormy day? Why was she picking on us, and why wouldn't she leave us alone?

When I did laundry in my wringer washer one day in mid-winter, *Gokum* came in the front door, without knocking, and plunged her hand into the rinse water. Talking rapidly in Cree, she grabbed a pail of hot water and dumped it into the rinse tub.

"But *Gokum*," I protested feebly, "I *like* to rinse my clothes in cold water." She didn't understand, or pretended not to.

After I hung my laundry on the clothesline and went back inside, I'd often see her adjusting a prop here and rehanging a towel over there.

"My *gokum* moved your sheets on the clothesline," the granddaughter said. "She didn't want them blowing against the tree."

I fumed about *Gokum* for the first few months, irritated at her for invading my life, wishing she would leave me alone. But by the time we left the reservation, three years later, I actually liked her. I knew then what she knew all along—I really had been ignorant about the First Nations culture and surviving in the North. She helped me in the way her people help each other, by seeing a need and meeting it without a lot of formalities.

Recently, I finally realized that the cat had done the same thing.

My sister and her husband and three boys came to visit us about a week after the cat first came to stay. Sleeping on the trampoline is a summer tradition at our house, and my two oldest nephews looked forward to it for months. At 10:30, before I went to bed, I took a flashlight out to the trampoline to check on them one last time. In the dim light I noticed an odd lump at the end of Jason's sleeping bag.

"It's that cat," he whispered, grinning. "It curled up by my feet."

Over their cereal the next morning the boys informed me that the cat ended up between their pillows, and every night the scene was repeated. No sooner would they settle down for the night than the cat would leap up on the trampoline and curl up, utterly contented at last, on their pillows.

"She slept by my head again, just like always," Keith said one morning. "This will be my best memory of this summer."

My sister and her family have left, but the cat is still here. She dozes under the car, catches mice in the fescue field, and meows only when she's hungry. She lets our 2-year-old color her back with blue sidewalk chalk. We are discussing names—Paul likes Holstein, Amy likes *Katz*, and Matt likes Daisy Mae. I went to Safeway and bought a bag of cat food, a big one.

Will she live long on this notorious corner? I wonder, anticipating the guilt. The cat twines around my ankles, reminding me that she came of her own free will, our children have a new pet to love, and two little nephews have warm memories of a furry Holstein cat hopping on the trampoline to keep them company in the dark.

Maybe what she was telling me so plaintively, when she first came, is that we needed a cat, and we didn't know it. But she did, and here she was, ready to meet that need in the only way she knew how.

Often, the things we don't know we need come into our lives without knocking.

Turning Forty

I'm going to be 40 on Saturday.

My mother told me the story of my birth every year when I was a child, how she knew I'd soon be here and Aunt Vina was rushing her to the hospital. The car kept getting hot, Mom would recall, and they had to stop three or four times to put water in the radiator.

They pulled in at one farm where a slow, talkative man wanted to discuss the crops and the weather. Vina grabbed the bucket from his hand, dashed to the pump, filled the bucket, dumped it in the radiator, and roared off, leaving the bewildered farmer behind.

And I was born just minutes after they reached the hospital. Another daughter, Mom would say. She couldn't believe how fortunate she was.

Now, approaching my birthday, it seems that turning 40 is something to dread, dismal and inevitable, somewhere between a disease and a curse.

"I'm 39 and holding," women tell me, grimacing. Party decorations for 40-year-olds are heavy on somber colors, gravestones, and banners shouting, "Over the hill!" My daughters giggle over the birthday cards at WinCo, all of which imply that next week my teeth will fall out. A bumper sticker announces, "I'd rather be 40 . . . than pregnant."

Most of all, I hear that mysterious phrase, "Life begins at 40."

It showed up recently at my sister-in-law's party, in blue icing on top of her cake. "What was it before then?" she wondered.

That saying also appeared, ironically, at my grandmother's funeral almost 14 years ago. Even if she knew what an identity crisis was, Grandma would never have bothered to have one, especially about turning 40. Her position in the family grew more powerful with each year, and she was as proud of her age as an Amish woman lets herself get about anything. When she was in her 90s we'd get postcards from her in her spidery handwriting. "I went to the John T. Yoder reunion in Buchanan County. There were 128 people there, and I was the oldest one."

Amish sermons—long, German, and preached without notes—often wander down unexpected rabbit trails. "Our deceased sister lived to be almost 104," the first preacher said at Grandma's funeral. "Now the *Englishers* have a saying, 'Life begins at 40,' because they don't like to grow older and they try to convince themselves it's not so bad. But we know that age doesn't really matter when it comes to serving God, and Sister Barbara served God for many years both before and after she was 40."

"Life begins at 40" was the only English phrase in that entire 45-minute sermon, and the only thing that my husband, bored and uncomfortable on the backless benches, understood.

It was also the only thing the second preacher had understood. A Dunkard from a neighboring church, he looked Amish but didn't speak German, and was asked to preach for the benefit of the *Englishers,* like my husband in the audience.

"I noticed that our brother thinks that life begins at 40," he said, halfway through his half-hour sermon. "But I believe I disagree with him. That is something that worldly people say because they don't like to grow older and they try to convince themselves it's not so bad. But we all know . . . ."

He went on to repeat what the first speaker said, thinking he was saying the opposite. Ever since, I have associated turning 40 with a vague sense of pathetic miscommunication.

Watching a stream of friends and relatives approach this milestone, I came to associate it most of all with a powerful restlessness.

"I have this longing for a baby girl," my sister e-mailed from Yemen a few years ago. "I love my three boys, I'm happy with them, this would not be a good time or place to have a baby . . . but I still have this incredible longing for a girl."

My sister-in-law, Bonnie, burst into the church nursery one Sunday and announced, "I'm going to open a bakery and go into foster care!"

We all looked at her, dumbfounded.

"I've felt so restless for the last year, and last week I decided what I'm going to do."

We all thought, *She's turning 40.*

"I want to do something *bad*," my brother's wife Geneva wailed on the phone. "I was always so good when I was a teenager," she went on, "and now I have this terrible urge to do something bad."

Thankfully, I've seen all of these women emerge intact on the other side of 40. Becky went back to work as a nurse instead of having another baby. Bonnie had another baby instead of opening a bakery. And Geneva managed to keep on being good until the urge to be bad disappeared.

So far, the restlessness hasn't reached me, but I expect it to hit when my youngest child goes to school. But I still face the realities of growing older, of no longer being young in a world that values youth above wisdom. Paradoxically, we all want to live a long time, but we don't want to grow old.

Often, I find, the noisiest voices in our culture have the most damaging messages, and the voices that I strain to hear speak the most truth.

"Gray hair is a crown of splendor," the Bible says, quietly nudging my conscience as I carefully isolate and pluck another wiry gray strand.

"You're going to celebrate, aren't you?" my friend Anita asks me.

Celebrate? No one had ever asked me that question, and it hadn't occurred to me to celebrate. Anita, it turns out, loves birthdays, loves to celebrate the years, loves to tell people how old she is.

"The older I get, the more I feel like I can be who I was meant to be," she says.

My friend Marilyn was a celebrating sort of person who laughed a lot, silently, her shoulders bobbing up and down. As I recall, she was too busy trying to stay alive to agonize about her approaching fortieth birthday. She was in remission one summer evening, her hair grown in short and curly after chemotherapy, when I saw her sitting on the front steps watching her 2-year-old daughter prancing on the sidewalk in her new summer sandals. Marilyn was laughing, oblivious to me, absorbed in this beautiful child skipping back to her, over and over, and announcing proudly, "I have new sandals, Mom!"

Four months later, Marilyn was dead, just days before she would have been 40 years old.

It may be a wild ride, and I might have to stop now and then to refill the radiator. But I've decided to listen to the quiet voices telling me to celebrate turning 40. I'll do it in honor of Marilyn, who never had the chance.

Ordinary Days

And someday, for Grandma's sake, I'll write a post card in spidery handwriting, "I went hiking in Switzerland. There were 25 of us, and I was the oldest one there."

Judgment Day

Glancing slyly around the courtroom, I compared myself to the others, wondering if I had any chance of impressing the judge.

Let's see. I'm older and more conservative than the neon-striped eyebrows, younger and skinnier than the plump polyester, better dressed than all the baggy khakis, more pious-looking than the gray ponytail.

Then, my conscience yanked me back to the truth. I was guilty. Despite my appearance, I knew I was guilty, guilty, guilty of driving 44 miles per hour in a 25 mile-per-hour zone in Philomath on June 23. And I was about to be judged.

June 23 was the last day of a family reunion in the Coast Range near Logsden. My husband Paul and our oldest son Matt had left early to get back to the warehouse and harvest, and I had a frustrating morning. The sausage-and-egg casserole burned when I made breakfast for the whole crowd. My 16-year-old daughter Amy was sick in bed and vomiting into a wastebasket. And I had to pack up with the reluctant help of two younger children who kept drifting off to play basketball.

We finally left with four of our children and two nephews. Half an hour later, I stopped along the narrow road to let Amy throw up. At noon, we reached Philomath. I bought gas while Amy moaned and the other kids complained of being hungry. Should I take time to buy lunch, I asked them, or cook something at home?

"Please, let's just go home," Amy begged, reclining in the front seat with agony in her eyes and her hand on her stomach.

"We can wait," the others said, generously.

Just before we passed Dairy Queen, I saw, at the same time, the police car and the speed-limit sign, and knew this was the final stroke of awfulness on an awful morning.

"You were going 44 in a 25 zone," the policeman said, smiling. "But if you show up in court, the judge is likely to reduce your fine if you have a good record. It's here in Philomath on the 13th of July." He handed me a yellow paper and left.

One hundred seventy-five dollars! Heavy-hearted, I drove home, put Amy to bed, cooked macaroni and cheese for the others, and burst into tears telling Paul about my morning.

Counting on the policeman's word that the judge would be lenient, I decided to appear in court rather than pay the fine by mail.

For the next few weeks, the impending court date dangled like a spider at the edge of my vision. I pondered the heavy theology of it all, of sin, guilt, and judgment to come.

What would it be like? Maybe it was a mistake not to watch TV all these years, since surely those courtroom shows would have given me some idea of what to expect.

My family tried to be helpful. "Be sure not to chew gum," 14-year-old Emily offered. "It's not respectful. At least that's what Randy said."

Randy is her Sunday-school teacher, known for letting the discussion wander down rabbit trails.

Amy instructed, "Don't forget to tell him you had a sick daughter and hungry kids. Make sure he knows you went 20 years without being stopped."

Emily said, "Maybe you shouldn't, because he'll think you're bragging."

Another day, Amy told me, "I have a verse for you, Mom. I found it this morning. 'When you are brought before . . . rulers and authorities, do not worry about how you will defend yourselves or what you will say, for the Holy Spirit will teach you at that time what you should say.'"

"But what about the little speech you told me to prepare about my sick daughter and hungry kids?"

Amy didn't know. That was between me and the Holy Spirit.

"Panty hose," said Geneva, my sister-in-law. "Don't wear denim. Something nice."

I chose a summery lavender dress I bought at St. Vincent de Paul.

"*That?*" Amy said. "Isn't that way too dressy?"

"It makes me feel confident. That's what matters."

At the Philomath town hall, I signed in at a table in the back of the courtroom, where a woman in a denim skirt—so much for Geneva's advice—handed me a form and told me I'd be third in line.

I found a seat on one of the dirty, cream-colored chairs and listened to the conversation behind me between Gray Ponytail and Baggy Khaki.

"This your first time?" the older man asked.

"No, I got a 37 in a 25 zone one time, and a 45 in a 25, a 75 in a 55, a 94 in a 65, a failure to stop, and a failure to use turn signal. Got my license suspended a couple times."

"Whoa, man. You need some liposuction on that heavy foot."

I smiled, comparing his record and mine. And then my smugness evaporated as a young clerk announced, "Judge Larry Blake. All rise."

A large man in a sweeping black robe strode in, and I went weak with fear, awe, and sudden visions of Judgment Day. All have sinned, the Scriptures say, and I was guilty.

The judge sat behind a raised platform, whacked his gavel, and told us to sit down at the table in the order we signed in. We could plead guilty, not guilty, or no contest, and then we would have a chance to say something.

Plump Polyester was second. Honest, she didn't see the person in the crosswalk until it was too late to stop.

"Okay," the judge said briskly. "Pick up this form and come in two weeks to discuss this further."

My turn. I sat at the table. "How do you plead?"

"Guilty."

"What do you have to say?"

I plunged in. "I know I'm guilty but I would like to ask for mercy because I haven't been stopped in 20 years and I've learned my lesson and (breathlessly) I had six children with me that day and five were hungry and my daughter was sick and I had to stop and let her throw up and (cue for pitiful Bambi eyes) I just wanted to get *home*.

"Hmmm," he said. "Kid throwing up. That's about as mitigating as you can get."

He paused. "All right. I'll reduce the fine." Then, surprisingly, he reminisced a bit. "I have three kids myself, and I remember one time, two of them were screaming in the back seat and I wanted to get home so badly, I would have driven through floods to get there."

The judge smiled. Smiled! I rose and took the paper from the young clerk. In the back, with my hands still shaking, I wrote a check for $130 and handed it to the woman in denim.

Neon Eyebrows, meanwhile, was at the table pleading no contest. The judge snapped, "I find you guilty."

I, on the other hand, was absolved, forgiven, and no longer guilty. I stepped into the sunshine, and pondered a generous theology of mercy and forgiveness.

Then, I drove to the ARC, my favorite second-hand store, where the quiet aisles soothed me for the next half hour. A vanilla cone at Dairy Queen completed my recovery and I got in the car and drove away, east on that long highway through Philomath, heading home. Slowly.

Panic and Pears

*W*e were almost ready to leave for school that Tuesday morning when we heard the news of the terrorist attacks on the East Coast.

I will never forget that image of my family in a frozen semicircle in the living room, listening to the radio. The older children stood motionless in their new school uniforms, lunch boxes in hand, and the only movement in the room was 2-year-old Jenny, oblivious to the horror, flitting around us.

I was in a daze the rest of the day. *Life ought to stop and wait, I thought. How could the sun keep shining, and how could our neighbor possibly be out there plowing the field next to our house?*

I heard my husband talking on the phone, "Your intermediate ryegrass came in at 95 percent, and then I got your last two purities and . . . ."

"Please stop," I wanted to say. "Give me time to catch up."

I have always been a worrier, seeing incurable cancer in every lump and picking out songs for my husband's funeral when he is late coming home. If the phone rings at midnight, it means my mother had a heart attack. So, when this tragedy struck, I immediately thought of the worst possible consequences.

The future, which had looked safe and promising the day before, suddenly seemed full of frightening possibilities.

War, more terrorist attacks, economic collapse. I began to worry, not for myself, but for all the loved ones that I felt responsible for—my five children, and my parents, both in their eighties. How could I protect them?

A box of pears had sat ripening in my kitchen for several days. They were given to us, and in happier days I may or may not have bothered to can them. But now it suddenly seemed that the future fate of all my loved ones rested in this silly box of pears, and, by hook or by crook, I was going to preserve them.

Canning pears is labor-intensive work, best undertaken with a group of children or friends to help. I was home alone with Jenny, but I grimly attacked the job. I gathered the jars, washed the pears, and prepared the sugar syrup, convinced I was somehow protecting my family from hunger, war, famine, disease, and pain.

I cut the pears in half, cored them, and peeled them. Pears are slippery, and peeling one is like giving a minnow a bath. My frustration mounted as they kept slipping out of my hands and splashing back into the water.

My Sunday-school teachers used to tell us that all the Bible verses we memorized would come back to encourage us in difficult times. If ever I needed encouragement, it was then. As I worked on the pears, odd verses popped from my feverish mind, like wads of stuffing coming out of holes in an old pillow.

"In those days was Hezekiah sick unto death."

"As vinegar to the teeth and smoke to the eyes, so is a sluggard to those who send him."

Those verses didn't help me a bit.

The first jar was barely half full when the phone rang. Curling brown shreds clung to my fingers as I rushed to wash my hands and get to the phone in time. Then I was back to work, warding off all the terrible unknowns that threatened my family. Cut, core, peel, drop it in the jar.

Jenny climbed on a chair beside me and tried to climb onto the table. I set her back down, but soon she was up on the chair again, sticking her fingers into the sugar syrup.

Cold water dripped from my wrists, Jenny kept getting in my way, and the phone kept ringing. Yet I felt compelled to keep on, pushing against the darkness that seemed to surround everyone I cared for.

"Read to me, Mom," Jenny begged, pushing against my legs.

"Later, Honey," I said. "Please, just go play." Why couldn't she understand that I was doing this for her good, for her future, for all of us?

Jenny left, but only for a minute, then she was back, hugging my legs, her brown eyes pleading. "Read to me, Mom. Please?"

Finally, I laid down my knife, washed my hands, and admitted defeat. It was no use. This wasn't about pears at all, but about my own helplessness. The raw truth was that I was powerless to protect my family, and all the pears in the world couldn't shield them against the terrible shadowy dangers we faced. Even the burst of national unity in the country, inspiring as it was, failed to reassure me.

I held Jenny on my lap and reached for *Old Hat, New Hat.* As I droned halfheartedly about all the different hats, suddenly the promises I needed began to march, unbidden, through my mind, one by one, orderly and appropriate.

"I am with you always."

"God will meet all your needs."

"Perfect love drives out fear."

"I sought the Lord, and he heard me, and delivered me from all my fears."

A few days later, my neighbor called and wondered if I wanted the grapes left on her vine. "I'm guessing there's enough for 10 or 15 quarts of juice," she said.

I told her I'd take all she had.

The grapes were so thick on her vine that we only picked half of them, filling two big bowls, a box, and two buckets. I took them home and processed them, jar after jar of rich purple juice crowding my kitchen counters, 44 quarts in all. I saw them not as my desperate defense against calamity, but as rich provision from God, affirmation that God was taking care of us.

Since then, the sun has been coming up every morning, our neighbor planted his field, and my husband continues to discuss seed-test results on the phone. I bought a package of tulip bulbs to plant beside the house.

And when I honestly acknowledge my own helplessness, I find that I am least afraid of the future.

Escapes

I am tempted sometimes to think that happiness can be found in recreation, freedom from responsibility, and self-indulgence. But any break from daily duties soon outlives its usefulness, and I come to realize that it is the routine itself, the work and service and sacrifice, that ultimately has the most value and satisfaction.

The first few weeks of June brought me a long, much-needed vacation. With all the end-of-school activities in May, my calendar was so full that appointments were spilling into the margins. I felt like a dispatcher at Sherman Brothers Trucking—answering the phone; delegating jobs; and making sure that the drivers had cars, the non-drivers had rides, and the under-10s had supervision.

In addition, everyone needed clean clothes to wear every morning and a hot supper to sit down to together at 6 p.m.

There are women who thrive on activity and having 50 things going on at once, but I am not one of them. I enjoy silence and staying at home and my own little rituals, things that don't normally occur with five children in the house. So when people asked me how I felt about more than half the family leaving for two weeks, I confided, "You know, I feel really guilty about this, but I'm looking forward to having them gone."

Paul and our two oldest daughters left for Mexico one morning after school was out to visit our church's missionaries, a yearly duty for Paul as the church's missions committee chairman. A few days later, Matt, our oldest son, left with his Aunt Barb, a new doctor beginning an internship in Pennsylvania. She had invited Matt and his cousin Keith to help drive her car and a U-Haul trailer to her new home.

So I was alone in an empty, echoing house with our two youngest, 9-year-old Ben and 4-year-old Jenny, both easy and amiable children with none of the angst or social lives or appetites of teenagers.

Every evening, I went through the entire bedtime routine with Jenny—jammies, snack, story, prayers, and bed. I could read *Bedtime for Frances* from start to finish with no phones ringing and no one hollering "Mom!" from the kitchen.

On hot afternoons, I sat outside and read while Jenny played in her wading pool. I discovered that Ben had never learned to play Andy-Over so I taught him, he and I on opposite sides of the lambs' shed, tossing a ball up and over, up and over. I took the children shopping and Ben took all the time he wanted comparing sweatbands at Footlocker.

No one was at home impatiently expecting supper before they were off to a meeting or basketball game. I stopped in at CG's Market in Harrisburg and bought a single gallon of milk. It lasted for days and days.

One night, we all slept outside on the trampoline. As the sun set, I turned off the lights in the house and then tucked Jenny into her little sleeping bag, my every move making the trampoline bob like a ship at sea.

I made sure Ben had his flashlight with him in his sleeping bag, then I settled down into mine. Jenny was soon sound asleep. Ben rambled on about basketball statistics for a few minutes, then he, too, fell asleep.

I curled up in my sleeping bag and felt like I was a good mom at last, breaking out of my routine and taking the time to do this. The fewer children I have, the better a mom I am,

I decided. Just think of how awesome a mom I could be if I didn't have any children at all.

It was not a restful night. The temperature dipped into the low 40s and the trampoline turned out to be hard and uncomfortable. Katzie the cat kept climbing over us, pushing gently but firmly with her paws like a midwife feeling for the baby's position.

The next morning, as Jenny said, "We had cat feathers all over our sleeping bags."

But the sun shining through the trees cheered me up, and I had another blissful day ahead of me with no school or deadlines or places I had to go.

One day, my sister-in-law and I found babysitters and went out for lunch, lingering over iced tea for the most relaxed time of "girl talk" I'd had in months.

I thought wistfully, at times, that it would be nice if my life could always be this stress-free. Yet, as pleasant as those weeks were, I didn't want them to last forever, and I was happy to pick up Matt at the airport and to see Paul and the girls drive in.

My calendar rapidly filled up, with dentist appointments and birthday parties again spilling over into the margins. The house is noisy again, full of ringing phones and slamming doors. I buy three gallons of milk at once, wash two or three dishwasher loads a day, and get up at 6 a.m. if I want a cup of tea in peace and quiet.

But this, after all, is reality and substance, my work and purpose and ministry. This is where the rewards are found, the greatest challenges and the greatest satisfaction.

I might feel like a better mom with fewer children at home, but if I didn't have any I wouldn't be a mom at all—"Duh!" as my kids would say. Good moms not only read all the way through *Bedtime for Frances,* they also tackle the unpleasant jobs such as insisting that their teenagers clean up after themselves in the kitchen and come home by curfew.

A week after everyone was home again and everything was wild and busy, I had an unexpected break, much shorter this time but just as refreshing.

One evening after Paul had spent the day cleaning out bins in preparation for harvest, he wondered if I'd like to go for a canoe ride. I hadn't canoed in years, and immediately took him up on his offer.

Muddy Creek is just across the road, so we didn't have far to go, yet it was like stepping out of my familiar universe and into another dimension as we pushed off from the creek bank, slipped into that quiet green tunnel of trees, and floated along below the level of Powerline Road and the ripening grass-seed fields.

We saw the neighborhood from an entirely new perspective—tombstones in the old cemetery pointed bravely toward the sky, and who knew that Leroy and Anita next door had solar panels on their garage roof? Noises were muffled, the slight swish of the paddles competing with a bird's sudden twitter or the splash of a nutria.

It was tempting to stay there forever, but before long it was time to turn around and go home. I had a fresh boost of energy as I cleaned up the kitchen and put children to bed.

As an escape from my routine, relaxing, shopping, and reading give me a new perspective and enable me to do my real work more effectively. Pursued for their own sakes, they become as pointless and unsatisfying as spending my life on Muddy Creek, endlessly paddling downstream.

The Gift
of an Ordinary Day

Yesterday was an ordinary day.

I brushed and braided my daughters' hair and drove the children to school, then stopped in to visit an elderly friend. After school, Amy, our 12-year-old, checked out an 18-inch stack of books from the library in Harrisburg. Second-grader Ben emptied the mousetraps and earned a quarter toward his next Lego set. Paul, my husband, figured out our taxes. Jenny, our busy toddler, unrolled six yards of toilet paper and dumped Cheerios on the floor. I helped 10-year-old Emily with her homework and wondered if she will ever quit making her A's look like O's. Matt, the tall teenager, poked me in the ribs to hear me shriek. That night, I snuggled next to my sleeping husband and listened to an owl hooting across the creek.

And I kept a promise I made seven years ago.

We lived in Canada then, near a camp for First Nations children and families, a hundred miles north of the Minnesota/Ontario border. With our four young children, we had traveled to Oregon for Christmas. On this particular night, January 16, 1994, we were on our way home and had only 25 miles to go. We were all tired of traveling and eager to get home after our 4,000-mile journey. Behind our van, we pulled the trailer that was to carry our belongings when we moved back to Oregon the following summer.

It was 10:30 at night and bitterly cold, probably 20 degrees below zero, with a light snow falling. The isolation of this hundred-mile stretch of road was unnerving enough in broad daylight, but at night it was almost hauntingly empty. We passed a gas station at the 40-mile mark; otherwise there was nothing but rocks, lakes, and trees. The last vehicle we had seen was a car we met just after we crossed the border almost two hours before.

Paul was driving, and the children slept. We felt safe and cozy, close together in the warm van, pushing a huge ball of light ahead of us through the darkness and the falling snow, mile after mile.

I saw it first, a shape appearing out of the darkness. A young bull moose trotted down the middle of the road ahead of us, hemmed in by guard rails on both sides. Paul stepped on the brakes and the van slipped and swerved on the snowy road. But we were unable to stop and we hit the moose with a gentle thump, like bumping your grocery cart into the one ahead of you at Safeway.

The van lurched and slid but stayed on the road. Paul eased the van on down the road a few hundred yards, where the guardrail ended and he could pull off the road. We checked to make sure everyone was okay, and Paul got out to inspect the van.

"It's not damaged that badly," he said when he came inside. "We hit it by the headlight, and the fan might be pushed in a little bit, but I'm going to leave the engine running to keep it warm in here. I think I'll go back and make sure that moose is off the road. Watch this gauge here, and if it starts to get hot, turn the engine off." He pulled on his fur hat and mitts, and left.

I sat in the driver's seat to watch the gauge, feeling calm and unafraid. Paul would soon be back and we would get home safely. After a while, I smelled something hot, just a whiff. I checked the gauge; it was fine. "I'm going to look at the engine," I told the children, who were now awake.

When I peered under the hood, nothing seemed abnormal. I walked on around to the passenger-side door of the van, opened it, and froze in shock and horror as I saw little flames shooting out of the dashboard. I couldn't think or move. Then, like a slide coming into focus on a screen, I was able to think one clear thought at a time.

Fire.

This van is on fire.

I've got to put it out.

I grabbed a sports bottle of milk by my feet and squeezed it at the fire. Nothing happened, but I inhaled black smoke that burned all the way down.

A new thought: *I've got to get my children out.*

Three-year-old Emily appeared in front of me, and I carried her out and waded through the snow to set her on the trailer behind the van.

Another thought, another child. I lifted out Amy, age 5, then Matthew, 7.

Another slide appeared on the screen in my mind.

My baby.

I reached through the billowing, burning smoke and unbuckled 5-month-old Benjamin's car seat. I pulled him toward me, grabbed his blankets, and waded back to set him on the trailer with the others.

As I did, I heard my children screaming: terrible, terrified screams that were swallowed up by the endless night and cold. And I realized I was alone, all alone with these helpless children in a world of malevolent horror, blackness, and flames. Paul was gone and we were the only people left in the world.

Another thought penetrated my dazed mind: *It's cold. I've got to keep my children warm.*

I yanked open the back door of the van. There on top was the big suitcase with their boots, ski pants, and extra wraps. That morning it had been heavy and bulky. Now, I pulled it out and tossed it far down into the ditch as though it was a basketball. Then, with mindless determination, I dug for the extra blankets that I knew were in there somewhere. The flames were almost to the back seat, but I hardly noticed. I had to get the blankets or my children would freeze.

A voice called me; a breathless, rasping voice.

"Dorcas, run!"

I couldn't run. I hadn't reached the blankets yet. Paul appeared close to me.

"It's going to explode! Get Benjy! *We've got to run!*"

Oh, yes—that gas tank under the back seat. I had forgotten.

I grabbed Benjamin in his carseat, Paul carried Emily, and with Matthew and Amy we started running, into the night, away from the van.

For the first time, I actually felt the cold. I looked down and saw my shoes, sweater, and skirt. *I'm going to freeze to death,* I thought calmly, and kept running.

Suddenly, out of the endless darkness around us, lights appeared. They were real. Headlights. What vast, glorious relief to see a pickup truck pull up beside us and a man jump out. He welcomed us into the truck and set the children into the wide space behind the seat.

Ahead of us, the moose struggled to lift his head from the highway. Behind us, orange flames leaped from every window of the van. And in the warmth and safety, I counted our children, over and over and over.

Ordinary Days

The next evening, while Paul answered calls from friends and relatives, I sat on the living room floor and read to the children. I could think clearly again, and felt the full horror of our experience wash over me, again and again. At the same time, I was overwhelmed with a sense of gratitude and wonder: we were all there. All of us. Together, whole, warm, safe, and alive.

It was the first time I really sensed how closely we walk to death, and I had a new awareness of the preciousness of the people I love. Too often, I realized, I had taken my family for granted and complained that my life wasn't exciting. Now I began to understand that even the most ordinary moments are treasures, priceless and fragile. So I promised myself that I would never lose that sense of wonder or complain that my life wasn't exciting enough.

And last night, lying in bed and listening to the owl, I kept my promise and thanked God for the incredible gift of an ordinary day.

About the Author

*D*orcas Smucker, a mother of six and a Mennonite minister's wife, lives in a 95-year-old farmhouse near Harrisburg, Oregon. In addition to her normal responsibilities of pulling splinters, settling arguments, and mopping floors, she writes a column, "Letter from Harrisburg" for the Eugene, Oregon, *Register-Guard*. She also speaks to various groups, which she enjoys because everyone listens and no one interrupts.

Her interests and hobbies include reading, crafts, sewing, travel, and exploring the Internet.